A
Parent's
Guide to
MANAGING
CHILDHOOD
GRIEF

100 Activities for Coping, Comforting, & Overcoming Sadness, Fear, & Loss

Katie Lear, LCMHC, RPT, RDT

ADAMS MEDIA
New York   London   Toronto   Sydney   New Delhi

Adams Media
An Imprint of Simon & Schuster, Inc.
100 Technology Center Drive
Stoughton, Massachusetts 02072

First Adams Media trade paperback edition July 2022

ADAMS MEDIA and colophon are trademarks of Simon & Schuster.

For information about special discounts for bulk purchases, please contact Simon & Schuster Special Sales at 1-866-506-1949 or business@ simonandschuster.com.

The Simon & Schuster Speakers Bureau can bring authors to your live event. For more information or to book an event contact the Simon & Schuster Speakers Bureau at 1-866-248-3049 or visit our website at www.simonspeakers.com.

Interior design by Sylvia McArdle
Interior layout by Colleen Cunningham
Interior images © 123RF/solodkayamari, fourleaflover

Manufactured in the United States of America

2 2023

Library of Congress Cataloging-in-Publication Data
Names: Lear, Katie, author.
Title: A parent's guide to managing childhood grief / Katie Lear, LCMHC, RPT, RDT.
Description: First Adams Media trade paperback edition. | Stoughton, Massachusetts: Adams Media, [2022]. | Includes bibliographical references and index.
Identifiers: LCCN 2022002425 | ISBN 9781507218372 (pb) | ISBN 9781507218389 (ebook)
Subjects: LCSH: Grief in children. | Adjustment (Psychology) in children. | Parenting. | Parent and child.
Classification: LCC BF723.G75 L43 2022 | DDC 155.4/124--dc23/eng/20220308
LC record available at https://lccn.loc .gov/2022002425

ISBN 978-1-5072-1837-2
ISBN 978-1-5072-1838-9 (ebook)

CONTENTS

ACKNOWLEDGMENTS

So many people have contributed to the creation of this book, and I'm grateful for all of them. First off, I owe a huge debt of gratitude to Julia Jacques and her team at Adams Media for this opportunity, as well as their support and flexibility along the way. Thank you for making this book a pleasure to write!

I'd like to acknowledge the therapists whose research, ideas, and expertise have been foundational to my own understanding of childhood grief and grief therapy, including William Worden, Eliana Gil, Liana Lownstein, Kevin O'Connor, Violet Oaklander, Judith Cohen, Anthony Mannarino, and the clinicians at the Dougy Center.

I'd also like to thank the Evidence-Based Treatment Dissemination Center and the Kint Institute in New York, as well as Felicia Carroll and the West Coast Institute in California, for their training, which continues to inform my work.

Melanie K. Deal and Brittany Quinzi, both educators, generously lent their expertise on how children can navigate grief in schools. Jordan Carroll provided a valuable second set of eyes when she reviewed the manuscript through the lens of a fellow child therapist. Emma Backer was immensely helpful in guiding this first-time author through the ins and outs of publishing.

Thank you to my parents, Bill and Patty, for the many hours spent sitting on the floor and playing with me, much in the same way that I encourage in this book. Thank you also to Zoe Harrison, our nanny and friend, whose help has made it possible for this new mom to run a therapy practice and raise a child while still having time to write.

Thank you, Steve, for your encouragement and willingness to do more than your fair share of parenting and chores these past few months. And thank you, Elliot, for your sunny personality and generously long naps.

INTRODUCTION

As parents and caregivers, we try to protect our children as much as we can from the difficult parts of life. Sometimes, despite our best efforts, painful experiences find us anyway. Grief and loss are universal experiences. They affect all of us, regardless of our age, race, economics, or gender.

Although we hope that our children won't experience grief until they are older, childhood bereavement is more common than you might expect. Sadly, every year, thousands and thousands of children in the United States lose a parent or a grandparent caregiver. Many families who never imagined they'd find themselves in this situation now have to learn how to grieve alongside their children.

Many cultures are not very comfortable talking about death. It's hard enough for adults to discuss it with each other, let alone figure out how to broach the subject with children. You may wonder how much your young child really understands about death and dying. You might worry that discussing a loved one's death will further upset the child. If you were also affected by the death, it can be even harder to find the right words to comfort a child in the midst of your own grief.

Children learn about the world—even in difficult times—through play. You have probably seen your child repeat play scenarios over and over as they make sense of something new. For bereaved children, play-based activities are opportunities to understand their new normal, express their feelings, and heal. When you participate in play with your child, you're allowing them to feel safe, heard, and loved. In this book, you'll find over one hundred activities for kids aged five to eleven to help you and your child reconnect and work through feelings of grief together.

The activities in this book will guide you and your child toward building skills that help people of all ages to process grief. You'll find games, art projects, and hands-on exercises that promote such concepts as:

- ★ Learning about death in an age-appropriate way
- ★ Understanding and embracing a variety of grief responses
- ★ Finding safe outlets for sadness, anger, and fear
- ★ Alleviating feelings of guilt
- ★ Honoring a loved one's memory
- ★ Telling our own stories of grief and loss
- ★ Encouraging hope and dreams for the future

As a children's therapist, I regularly get to see how resilient children are. Kids can't help but keep growing and changing, even through hard times. With some loving support, they overcome incredibly difficult circumstances. Even if you didn't grow up feeling comfortable talking about death, you can help your children feel safe and supported when they share their own feelings. Giving your child something you didn't receive yourself is a huge gift.

You can't make grief go away or prevent children from hurting when a loved one dies. What you *can* do is help children learn to live through their grief, remember their loved one who died, and keep moving forward in life. My hope is that, over time, this period of grief becomes one chapter of a much longer story for you and your child.

ALL ABOUT GRIEF

This part of the book provides a foundation for understanding grief and how to talk about it with your child. Even though you don't need any special expertise to use the skills in this book, it will still help to understand grief and its impact on children before you begin. You'll come away from these chapters with some ideas and language you can use to begin conversations with your child.

Whether you are anticipating a death, have recently lost a loved one, or simply want to prepare for the future, you'll find information here to guide you. We'll talk about different types of grief and the many ways that grief can look and feel. You'll learn how children express grief at different ages so that you can better gauge how your child is coping.

If you're looking for immediate solutions for how to give or get support in the aftermath of a death, there are ideas for you in this part as well. We'll look at the ways you can set up supports for your child at school, at home, and in the community. You'll learn how to begin difficult conversations with your child about different kinds of losses and what you can do to help your child feel as safe as possible in the first few days following a death.

We'll also discuss how to help involve your child in the mourning process in a way that feels right for your family. If you're wondering whether or not your child should attend a wake, funeral, or memorial service, we'll weigh the pros and cons.

By the time you've finished this part, you'll have some preparation to help your child navigate the shock and chaos of early grief. You'll know what your child needs in order to begin healing, and when it will be most helpful to begin the activities in this book.

CHAPTER 1

WHAT PARENTS NEED TO KNOW ABOUT GRIEF

Grief is a subject many people don't get a chance to talk about before it happens to them. In this chapter, you'll learn some basics about grief and mourning that can guide the future work you do with your child. Grief is such a personal experience, and it can show up in so many different ways. You may understandably be concerned about whether the responses you are seeing from your child are typical. We'll talk about how a child's grief process is different than an adult's, and how different kinds of loss can lead to different types of grief.

You'll also find an age-by-age guide that explains how children from the preschool through tween years tend to understand and cope with death. Every child is an individual, but this general information can help you identify what concerns your child might be wondering about, and areas where they may need help from you to understand their loss. You'll gain an awareness of the many ways grief can show up in a child's emotions, behavior, and thinking. You'll also discover that "normal" grief can look many different ways and have a sense of situations that might lead to more difficult grieving. This background will guide you as you navigate this difficult time with your child.

WHAT IS GRIEF?

Grief is what we feel when we lose someone or something we care about. While you may hear people discussing grief as a response to major life changes like a divorce or a chronic illness diagnosis, when most of us think of grief, we think of death. Although it's sometimes used as a synonym for sadness or despair, grief actually encompasses a wide range of thoughts, feelings, and even bodily symptoms.

Grief affects each individual differently, but the experience of grief is universal. All human cultures grieve, and researchers have even found evidence of grieving among other animal species. As painful and terrible as grief may feel, it's a normal and healthy process. Anger, anxiety, and deep sadness are often a part of grieving, but grief by itself is not a mental health diagnosis. Grief is a sign that we're capable of forming relationships. It means we care about others, and we miss them when they are gone.

Usually, we use the word "grief" to describe a person's internal experiences after a death, such as their emotions, beliefs, and physical well-being. Mourning, on the other hand, refers to the way that grief is shown to the outside world, such as through funerals, rituals, and expressions of feelings. In this book, you will learn ways to help children cope with the feelings of grief as well as mourn their losses in child-friendly ways.

HOW COMMON IS CHILDHOOD GRIEF?

If you're the caregiver of a bereaved child, you may feel as though you're the only ones going through this life-altering event. However, childhood grief is more common than you might expect. According to a research tool called the Child Bereavement Estimation Model, as of 2021, one in fourteen American children will experience the death of a parent or sibling before the age of eighteen. That's 5.3 million children in the United States alone.

This model doesn't, however, consider the deaths of extended family or other important people in a child's life. Plus, a child's risk of losing a family member varies based on location, socioeconomic status, public health issues such as pandemics, and other factors. Nevertheless, the data is clear: Children grieving over the death of a loved one is not a unique phenomenon.

If you imagine that an average public school classroom holds about twenty students, there are likely other children within your child's school or even their grade who have experienced grief too.

DIFFERENT TYPES OF GRIEF

Grief can be divided into a few broad categories. As a caregiver, it can be helpful to be aware of the different ways grief can manifest, especially if your child has experienced a death that's particularly difficult or traumatic.

* **Anticipatory grief** happens when there is advance knowledge that a person will soon die, such as when someone gets a diagnosis of a terminal illness. In these cases, loved ones may begin their grieving process before the death has occurred.
* **Normal grief** refers to a grief process where there aren't complications that get in the way of mourning a loss. Children experiencing this kind of grief may be able to work through their feelings on their own, without needing professional help. However, "normal" doesn't mean that this kind of grief is not painful or difficult.

* **Masked grief** is grief that's held inside and not shown to others. The griever may try to be stoic or put on a happy face for others, but they are still hurting.
* **Traumatic grief** happens after a death that is very sudden or violent, such as deaths due to car accidents or crime. Children who experience traumatic grief are at risk of developing post-traumatic stress and may need extra help from a therapist.
* **Disenfranchised grief** can occur when a person's death carries a social stigma, such as a death by suicide or drug overdose. It can be hard for survivors to talk about these deaths with others or get the support they need.
* **Complicated grief** is what happens when a person is not able to resolve their feelings in the way they need to for reasons such as stress, lack of support, trauma, or difficulty talking about the death. Children experiencing this kind of grief tend to feel distress for longer periods, and it may get in the way of daily life activities. Therapy can help kids with complicated grief to heal.

ARE THERE REALLY "STAGES" OF GRIEF?

If you've heard anything about grief before, you've likely heard that it happens in stages. This idea was coined by Elisabeth Kübler-Ross, a psychiatrist and grief expert, in 1969. According to the Kübler-Ross model, the five stages of grief are:

* Denial
* Anger
* Bargaining
* Depression
* Acceptance

Thoughts about how grief works have changed over time. In recent years, we've learned that most people don't go through these stages in order. Grief is not linear, nor does it have a clear ending. While many grievers will experience these feelings, they may not experience them in order, and they will likely revisit some feelings over and over again.

Another psychologist, William Worden, believed that getting through grief requires more than just experiencing emotions; it's an active process that takes work. His Four Tasks of Mourning describe the challenges grieving people face as they come to terms with a death:

* Accept the Reality of the Loss
* Work Through the Pain of Grief
* Adjust to a World Without the Deceased
* Maintain a Connection with the Deceased While Embarking on a New Life

The activity chapters of this book incorporate ideas from both Kübler-Ross's stages and Worden's tasks. There is no set time line on when a person should complete these tasks or work through their feelings. You and your child can go through this book's activities at your own pace, in any order you feel is right.

CHILDREN GRIEVE DIFFERENTLY THAN ADULTS

It may be hard to believe now, but for a long time experts believed that children weren't capable of grieving! Of course, we know now that this is far from the truth. Even very young children—and infants—have powerful responses to the death of a loved one. However, children grieve differently than adults do, which can sometimes make their grief process more difficult to notice or understand.

In general, children tend to work through their grief in bite-sized pieces. You may notice that your child dips in and out of their feelings of grief, sometimes approaching the feelings head-on and other times pushing them away to focus on something else. While it would be jarring to see an adult crying one minute about a loved one's death and laughing and playing the next, this can be perfectly normal for children.

Some children will not have any outward response to their loss immediately following a death and may go about daily life almost as if nothing had happened. However, a child may be grieving even when those feelings aren't visible on the outside.

Children tend to work through trauma and loss more quickly than adults do. It's not unusual for children to be ready to talk about difficult subjects before the adults in their lives. However, just because a child has seemingly moved on doesn't mean their grief is finished. Children may revisit their grief as they grow up and understand the depth and permanence of their losses in new ways.

How a child grieves depends on their emotional and cognitive development and their ability to understand what death means, as well as an individual child's personality and life experiences. A child who is developmentally ahead or delayed compared to their peers may grieve in ways that are similar to an older or younger child.

HOW PRESCHOOLERS GRIEVE

At ages three and four, children aren't old enough to conceptualize death. While they may have the language to begin talking about it, it's too abstract of a concept to fully understand. Often, a child's understanding of death comes from movies or cartoons, which may not be realistic.

Children in this age range have a hard time understanding that death is permanent. They may imagine that a loved one has gone away, left them, or gone to sleep. They might worry that they, too, could get sick and die like their loved one.

When preschoolers are under stress, they often go back to behaviors from earlier developmental stages, which is called regression. This is an effort to get comfort and care from old habits when newer coping skills aren't enough to handle a situation. Bed-wetting, tantrums, separation anxiety, and thumb-sucking are all common signs of regression. With support from loved ones, many children will resolve these behaviors on their own in a short period of time.

Preschoolers tend to live in the present, and they worry a lot about their own safety and who will care for them. Young children learn through repetition, so you may hear many repeated questions following a death as your child tries to make sense of their world.

Make-believe play helps young children to understand new events and process their feelings about them. You may see children acting out play scenarios that have to do with death, such as dolls traveling to heaven or toys repeatedly dying during play. This can be surprising to adults, but it is usually a healthy sign that children are working through their grief.

HOW EARLY ELEMENTARY CHILDREN GRIEVE

Experts like William Worden suggest that five- to seven-year-olds may have a particularly tough time managing grief. This is because they are old enough to have some understanding of death, but are too young to have mastered the coping skills they need to handle the big feelings that accompany a loss.

If you have a child in this age range, you are probably used to hearing many "why" questions in everyday life. You can anticipate hearing lots of "why" questions about death and dying too, as children try to make sense of what has happened. Your child may still need some help understanding that death is permanent.

Children in this age range also tend to assume they're the cause of major events that happen around them. This type of thinking is a normal, healthy part of child development. It means that many younger kids are beginning to understand that their thoughts and feelings have a direct impact on others. But at this age, their understanding can go too far, and they imagine they have more of an impact than they really do. For example, they may think that having an angry thought about someone could lead them to get hurt in real life. This concept is called "magical thinking."

When a loved one dies, children may feel immense guilt or worry that they were somehow responsible for the death. It's important to educate young school-aged children about what does and does not cause a person to die.

Children in this age range may have big emotional responses to the death, while others may mask their feelings. It's still common to see changes in behavior, such as difficulty sleeping or eating. Acting-out behaviors like defiance and tantrums are common too, since it's so hard to put the feelings of grief into words.

HOW LATE ELEMENTARY CHILDREN GRIEVE

By ages eight to ten, children are more aware of cause and effect, and they understand that other people have thoughts and feelings that are different from their own.

They also have a deeper understanding of the finality of death. As a result, you may notice that your late elementary schooler moves in and out of their feelings of grief for longer periods than younger siblings or peers.

Although the era of "magical thinking" is over by this age, your child has a strong sense of right and wrong. They may still wonder about whether they or their loved one were somehow to blame for the death. Because older children are more attuned to their caregivers' emotions, they may try to take care of a surviving parent or avoid sharing negative emotions so as not to upset others.

Kids tend to take a lot of pride in their activities at this age and may throw themselves into hobbies, extracurriculars, and generally being busy as a way to avoid hard feelings. Regular amounts of activity can provide a healthy way of coping, since grief can sometimes be too overwhelming for children to process all at once. On the other hand, some children's grief may impact their ability to concentrate on activities or school or to get along with other children.

HOW TWEENS GRIEVE

Children ages ten and up are approaching puberty and young adulthood, which means their intellectual and emotional lives are increasingly complex. Tweens are old enough to fully understand death in a permanent and abstract way. The death of a loved one can trigger thoughts about their own mortality or worries about the mortality of others.

The older kids get, the more central friendships become to their lives. Children this age really want to fit in with a peer group, and close friends become a sort of second family outside the house. Kids with good social support systems may be able to lean on their friends while grieving, but caregivers may have a harder time encouraging tweens to open up at home.

Conversely, tweens may be very self-conscious about their grieving and worry about how their peers will perceive them if they know about the death. They may worry they're not grieving the right way or that their feelings are abnormal, especially if others around them have had different responses to the death.

Older kids are also more prone to coping in unhealthy ways such as self-harm or substance use. They are also at higher risk for suicidal thoughts, so caregivers should look out for risk factors.

DO BOYS AND GIRLS GRIEVE DIFFERENTLY?

Every child is different, but studies have found overall differences in how boys and girls tend to grieve. Boys are more likely to express grief through externalizing behaviors, meaning they act out their feelings. This might look like getting into fights at school, tantrums, difficulty following rules at home, or angry verbal outbursts.

Girls are more likely to express grief through internalizing behaviors, meaning they turn their feelings inward. This can make their symptoms more difficult to spot.

Children who internalize may experience depression and anxiety. They might also withdraw from social activities they used to enjoy, or struggle with attention or appetite.

GRIEVING AND THE RISK FOR FUTURE MENTAL HEALTH PROBLEMS

It's understandable to worry about the possible long-term effects of losing a loved one at a young age. Research has shown that children who lose an immediate family member, especially a parent, have a higher risk of developing mental health problems both during childhood and later in life.

If you're a caregiver of a bereaved child, this might sound very frightening. However, having an increased risk does not mean mental health problems are inevitable, or that they can't be overcome. Let's take a closer look at what the research says, and what it could mean for you and your child.

The Research

A 2018 study from the University of Pittsburgh's Department of Psychiatry followed children for seven years following the death of a parent. The children in the study were between seven and seventeen years old, and they were compared to peers who hadn't experienced a death. Compared to their peers, the bereaved children were twice as likely to be diagnosed with depression in the two years following the death. They were also more likely to be diagnosed with post-traumatic stress disorder (PTSD).

Although the risk of depression waned after the first two years, the bereaved children in the study continued to have more struggles with school, work, family, and romantic relationships for the entire seven-year period when compared to their non-bereaved peers. It's possible that the early depression and trauma may set these children up for difficulties down the road, even if they don't fully meet the criteria for a mental health diagnosis at older ages.

A number of other studies have found similar results, noting that bereaved kids are at increased risk for a wide range of mental health problems like anxiety, depression, behavior difficulties, and substance use in young adulthood. Notably, children who lost a parent to suicide are at increased risk of dying by suicide themselves in adulthood.

There Is Still Hope

While some children will struggle for a long time following a death, this isn't the case for every child. Many children will work through their grief without serious, long-lasting symptoms. What's more, it is also possible for children to change in positive ways following trauma and loss. Researchers are paying more attention to an emerging field called post-traumatic growth, which explores these possibilities. We'll talk more about post-traumatic growth in some of Chapter 10's activities.

The good news is that you can play an important role in how grief will affect your child. Many factors play into how vulnerable or resilient a child will be in the face of grief. While some of those factors aren't under your control, many are. Furthermore, many studies agree that getting a child therapeutic help in the short term can improve their mental health in the years to come. If you sense your child is struggling, therapy can be a valuable support in addition to this book.

WHAT RISK FACTORS MAKE CHILDREN VULNERABLE AFTER LOSS?

A number of circumstances can put children at higher risk for developing complicated grief, the type that can cause lasting difficulties if not addressed. Many of these risk factors aren't in your control and have to do with the nature of the death or the child's life before the death.

The Harvard Child Bereavement Study identified a number of traits that tended to put children at risk of more difficult outcomes following a death. In general, the categories at an increased risk are:

* Young children (younger than twelve)
* Girls of any childhood age
* Children who experienced a loved one's death before age eight

Additional risk factors included:

* A previous history of trauma or loss
* A sudden, unexpected, or violent death
* The death of a parent, especially a mother
* A strained or difficult relationship with the deceased loved one
* A previous history of mental health problems for the child or caregiver

While these factors are largely outside of a caregiver's control, there are some areas in which a child can be supported to reduce risk following a death. The study also found that a child's support system in the time following a death can be a source of either risk or resilience. Some factors that put a child at risk following a death included:

* A culture that discouraged expressing feelings of grief
* Low self-esteem
* Lack of support system
* Lack of opportunities to mourn the death

If your child has multiple risk factors for complicated grief, an evaluation with a counselor can help you determine whether or not therapy could help your child get some needed additional support. We'll discuss how to find a counselor in this book's final chapter.

WHAT HELPS CHILDREN BE MORE RESILIENT AFTER LOSS?

Research on childhood trauma and grief shows us that a child's environment plays a big role in how resilient a child will be in the face of adversity. We call these traits "protective factors" because they shield a child from some of the long-lasting side effects of trauma and loss.

A child's age, gender, and the nature of their loved one's death will all influence their grieving process—and we've established that you can't control these pieces of the puzzle. However, you do have some control over other factors, such as whether your child has:

★ A loving relationship with surviving parents or caregivers
★ Supportive role models outside of the home
★ Strong self-esteem
★ An abundance of positive family time
★ Consistent, healthy discipline
★ A stable homelife with limited stress

We also know that children cope best when their caregivers are coping well. If you are the parent or caregiver of a bereaved child, anything you do to support your own mental health and wellness will directly impact your child's recovery.

Consistency and nurturing contribute to a child's sense of felt safety: the assurance that they are in a secure place where they will be cared for. This security is one of the first steps toward healing. In the next chapter, we'll talk about how you can approach the first days and weeks of grieving with safety in mind.

CHAPTER 2

CREATING SAFETY AFTER LOSS

If you're dealing with a recent or impending death, you may be overwhelmed by everything that's about to happen. There will be a funeral to plan, financial decisions to make, and extended family to inform. It's an enormous task all by itself, but it is especially challenging when you also must help a young person navigate one of the most difficult life experiences. In this chapter, you'll get practical information about how to help your child—and yourself—through the first days, weeks, or months following the death of a loved one.

There's no one-size-fits-all prescription for grief; every family has different needs. This chapter will provide a general road map for how to move forward while giving your child a sense of emotional safety. You'll learn how to talk about death in kid-friendly terms, as well as concrete steps you can take to help your child feel secure as they begin to process their loss. We'll also talk about how to approach the activities in this book, and how to determine if your child is ready to begin talking and playing through their grief.

BEFORE A LOVED ONE DIES

If at all possible, begin talking about death with your child before they experience the loss of a loved one. Children who have a good understanding of death will have one less hurdle in front of them as they work through their grief processes. Using day-to-day examples, you can help your child learn that death is permanent, not usually anyone's fault, and a natural part of life.

A pet goldfish, a houseplant, and even roadkill are all entry points for these conversations. Describe the death in simple terms and model how to express feelings about it: "Our plant died. It's so sad when that happens." Allow your children to express curiosity about death and ask any questions that come to mind. Some activities from Chapter 3, such as Life-Cycle Drawing and Read a Grief Story, can help children learn general, age-appropriate information about death before they experience it firsthand.

TALKING ABOUT TERMINAL ILLNESS

If you know a loved one's death is near, speak directly about what is happening. You can let your child know that although their loved one is receiving the best medicine or care, sometimes those things unfortunately do not help cure an illness. Tell your child that when their loved one's body gets too sick to keep working, they will die.

Children benefit from a simple explanation of the illness and how it will impact their loved one's appearance and behavior. For example, if a loved one is undergoing chemo, it's helpful for kids to know what to expect.

You can also prepare your child for any possible changes in the family, such as parents needing to be away from home more often, or other family members stepping in to help take care of the child. Reassure your child that, no matter what, they will be cared for.

AFTER A LOVED ONE DIES: TALKING ABOUT DEATH

You may feel pressure to say or do exactly the right thing in order to protect your child's feelings when talking about a death. We don't have many opportunities to practice these kinds of conversations. Fortunately, you don't have to phrase things perfectly in order to help your child. No matter what vocabulary you use, showing up as your loving, genuine, honest self will make a world of difference.

It's important to speak to your child about the death as soon as possible. It can be tough for children to discover later on that they were among the last to learn of a loved one's death. Select a familiar, private space to talk where your child will have comfort items to lean on, such as toys, pets, or a favorite blanket. If talking at home is not an option, a friend's house or a counselor's office can also feel safe.

What Do I Say?

In the aftermath of a death, what children really need to know is:

* What happened?
* What does this mean for me?
* Who is going to take care of me?
* Are my feelings okay?

Start by letting your child know that you have something important to share that might bring up big feelings for them. Make sure you have your child's attention and eye contact before moving forward.

It sounds blunt to adult ears, but direct language like "dead" and "died" will help your child better understand what's happening. If you haven't discussed it already, share some basic information about your loved one's cause of death. Take your time, leaving room for your child's responses and questions.

After sharing the news, let your child know about what will happen next. Will anything change in their routine? Who will be taking care of them? What preparations will the family be making in the next few days? Reassure your child that no matter what, they'll be safe and cared for.

For younger children, consider a script like this one as a jumping-off point for this conversation:

I need to talk to you about something very important that has happened. It's something we are both going to have some big feelings about. Uncle John had a problem with his heart today. It stopped beating, which made his body stop working, and he died. When a person is dead, it means their body and brain stop working for good. It means Uncle John has stopped thinking and feeling, and we won't get to talk with him again. We will go over to Aunt Linda's tomorrow to see her and your cousins. I will be home with you tonight to take care of you, and Uncle Bobby is coming to visit too. He will help bring you to school. We will all be here if you need us.

Older children often have a better understanding of death. They may ask more questions about the cause of death or the circumstances surrounding it. As a rule of thumb, if your child is old enough to formulate a question, they are old enough to hear the answer, even if it's sad or uncomfortable. It's also okay not to have all the answers. Sometimes "I don't know" is the most honest response you can give.

Euphemisms like ˈwent home.ˈ ˈwent to sleep.ˈ and ˈpassed awayˈ seem kinder and gentler to us. but they can be confusing or frightening to children. They may cause children to wonder why their loved one decided to leave. or if they will also ˈfall asleepˈ and never wake up.

Before ending the conversation, come up with a care plan for the rest of the day. Help your child think of ways to care for themselves physically and comfort themselves emotionally. You can offer a few choices, such as watching a favorite movie together, cuddling on the couch, or spending time with a favorite pet or stuffed animal.

When the Cause of Death Is Difficult to Talk About
Caregivers sometimes wonder if they should share the cause of death with a child when the circumstances around the death are painful or hard to explain. Children don't need to know every detail, but a simple explanation can ease anxiety and pave the road for deeper knowledge as a child grows. Later in life, children will inevitably learn more details about the death, so it helps to plant those seeds of understanding now.

DEATHS FROM CANCER
Many experts suggest describing cancer as an illness that affects our cells. Consider saying something like "Nana had a disease called cancer that affects tiny parts of our

body called cells. Cancer makes cells grow really fast and turns good cells into bad cells. These bad cells can hurt the good cells and make a person very sick."

DEATHS FROM COVID-19

Chances are, your child has already heard a lot of information about coronavirus. However, they may also have heard misinformation that causes unhelpful or unnecessary fear about their own safety.

You can explain Covid-19 using language like "Many people are getting sick with a kind of germ called the coronavirus. Kids almost never get sick with coronavirus, and most grownups only get a little bit sick. Every once in a while, coronavirus makes a grownup very sick. It can give them fevers and make it very hard to breathe. If a grownup gets very sick with coronavirus, sometimes their lungs or other organs stop working, and they die."

DEATHS DUE TO SUICIDE OR VIOLENCE

These can be the most difficult deaths for adults to think about, let alone to explain to children. Even in these instances, age-appropriate information helps kids feel more secure in their knowledge of what happened. You can build on this understanding as your child grows.

For very young children, start with a simple description of what physically caused the death, such as "He accidentally got very hurt and died" or "She took too much of a medicine, and it made her body stop working."

For older children, addiction and depression can be explained in more detail: "Sarah had a disease called depression that affected her brain and made her feel so sad that she could not think clearly. Sometimes depression tricks people into thinking that they can't get help to feel better, and it makes the person not want to be alive anymore."

WHEN A CHILD DIES

When the unthinkable happens and a child dies, it can be incredibly difficult to figure out what to say to a surviving child. This is particularly true if your child has lost a sibling, cousin, or close friend.

If the child endured a long illness, you might start by saying, "We all hoped that Liam would get better, but his body was too sick." Emphasize that nothing your child said, thought, or did could cause this death to happen. Sometimes, children mistakenly believe that their anger, jealousy, or negative thoughts toward a sibling could have caused their death. Saying something like "Liam's death was not anybody's fault, and nothing we said or did caused him to die" is a good first step toward addressing this kind of guilt.

Finally, if a child has lost a sibling, the whole family will be grieving intensely. Find adults in the extended family or community who can provide extra support so parents have the time and space they need to grieve.

BE PREPARED FOR A VARIETY OF REACTIONS

Some kids appear to have no reaction at all to news about a death, while others become visibly upset and need extra comfort and reassurance right away. Your child may move quickly between different feelings, seemingly grieving one minute before moving on to another activity the next. Any of these reactions are normal and healthy. Children process this heavy information differently than adults, and it's not unusual for them to take it one small step at a time.

After you tell your child about the death, you may notice younger children asking you the questions again and again. Children learn through repetition, and hearing the same response to their questions is comforting. Let your child know that any question—even small or silly ones—are okay to ask.

Children can learn factual information about death right alongside spiritual beliefs. Ensure your child understands the finality of death first, and then share your family's views about the afterlife. For example, you can tell your child: "Grandma died, which means her body stopped working, her heart stopped beating, and her soul went up to Heaven. Death means Grandma's soul can't come back from Heaven, and so we won't be able to see her or talk to her anymore. It's okay to be sad about that." This helps your child understand their loved one can't return from Heaven.

GETTING SUPPORT FROM FAMILY AND FRIENDS

You will likely hear many offers for help and support in the overwhelming days following your loved one's death. People who make comments like "let me know what I can do" mean well, but it may feel too difficult to delegate tasks, or even figure out what you really need. Consider asking one friend to serve as a point person to field phone calls and texts, organize food drop-offs, and help make these decisions.

You or your point person can assign concrete tasks to these well-intentioned helpers. Consider asking for assistance with household chores such as groceries, yard work, and childcare. Organizing a meal train is another great way to channel people's impulse to be helpful into something actionable and useful.

Getting Support from Your Child's School

Most schools have a lot of experience helping children cope with the loss of parents, teachers, and peers. They likely have protocols in place already to help grieving children. Contacting your child's guidance counselor and letting them know what has happened is a good place to start.

It's often helpful for children to get back into the routine of school, where life feels more "normal" and they have the support of friends. Before your child returns, talk with the school to decide whether a counselor should prepare their class for the return. One or two close friends approaching a child about the death can be a comfort, but getting comments from everyone could be overwhelming.

Your child's teacher should be informed of the death. This way, they can be sensitive to any upcoming events in the curriculum that might be triggering, such as Father's Day activities or assignments to interview a grandparent. Your child can work with their counselor to come up with a plan for these kinds of events that feels right to everyone.

You can also ask for accommodations to help your child get through the early days following a death. Some schools have different options available; here are a few you can advocate for if you feel they'd be helpful for your child:

* A shortened school day or later start time as your child readjusts
* Temporary academic accommodations, such as more time on tests
* The option to visit a counselor or call a loved one during difficult moments
* An alternative location to eat lunch—sometimes a boisterous room full of happy kids can be a lot for a grieving child to take in
* Permission to bring a comfort object to school

You can also ask about joining a peer support group for grieving children. If your school has one available, it can be extremely helpful and validating for your child. If a group is not available, your counselor may have recommendations for other options.

Getting Support from Your Community

If a grief group at school isn't an option, there are likely community organizations near you that can help children and families through grief. The Dougy Center's website (www.dougy.org) has a searchable database to help you find local grief support groups. Hospices are often knowledgeable about nearby services as well.

Support groups can benefit both grieving kids and adults. Grief is isolating, especially if you do not have friends who have experienced similar losses. Kids may feel that their peers don't understand them. Without the examples of other grieving children, they may worry their feelings are wrong or inappropriate. You may also benefit from talking to other caregivers who are a little ahead of you in their grief process, who can speak to you honestly and from personal experience.

SHOULD MY CHILD ATTEND THE FUNERAL?

Caregivers may wonder whether it's appropriate for young children to attend a funeral or wake. Will the sight of a loved one's dead body be traumatic for a child? What if family members are openly crying or very emotional—will that frighten them? Will a child's behavior be disruptive at a time when adults are trying to grieve?

If a child wants to attend the funeral, the benefits usually outweigh the drawbacks. Talk about what your child will see and experience at the funeral in advance so they don't encounter any surprises. If there will be an open casket, prepare your child for how their loved one's body will appear. The Toy Funeral activity in Chapter 3 may be a good entry point for this conversation.

Help your child feel included by giving them a special job, such as selecting flowers or a song for the service. Have a contingency childcare plan in place for younger children who may not be able to handle the entire event. You might plan to have the child stay only for a limited time, asking a friend to bring the child home if they decide they've had enough.

If a child does not want to attend a funeral, they shouldn't be forced to go. You can find another way to memorialize your loved one together at home, such as lighting candles, singing a song together, or looking at old photo albums. If the funeral is streamed online, watching a portion of the ceremony together may be a good compromise.

REESTABLISHING SAFETY IN THE "NEW NORMAL"

Consistent routines, warm relationships, and a caregiver's attitude help children regain a sense of safety and normalcy after a loved one dies. As your family begins to adjust, adding gentle structure, opportunities to connect, and self-care back into your day can go a long way toward building your child's resilience.

Routines

It's normal for things to feel out of sync in the days following a death. Returning to some basic routines as soon as you're able will help children cope and allow them to regain their sense of safety. Young children rely on routines to feel secure. Being able to predict what will happen next offers a sense of security in a world that can otherwise seem chaotic or confusing.

You don't need to strictly regiment every moment of the day, however. Instead, focus on a few daily activities like meals, daycare, playtime, and bedtime. Making a visual schedule can help younger kids anticipate when these activities will occur and make transitions easier.

One-on-One Attention

You may also want to set aside time each day when your child can look forward to individual, playful attention from you. Research shows that even ten minutes of one-on-one time a day can help meet a child's emotional needs, making them less likely to act out in other ways. There's no need to plan a big outing or buy a special toy: A few minutes drawing together or following your child's lead as they play is enough.

Self-Care for Caregivers

Prioritizing your own well-being isn't selfish. In fact, it's one of the most helpful things you can do for your child. Kids look to their caregivers to decide how they should think, feel, and respond in new and stressful situations. By tending to your own emotions, you'll be showing your child a model of what healthy grieving looks like.

This doesn't mean you have to put on a happy face or be relentlessly positive around your children while you are grieving. Showing your own feelings of sadness, anger, and worry gives kids permission to do the same. When you demonstrate how you're coping, your child will learn by example that they can cope too.

Any healthy activity that gives you an outlet for your feelings or provides a break from thinking about grief is valid self-care. Journaling, talking to a trusted friend, or seeking therapy can all help you to process emotions. Time away from your children, exercise, and social activities can provide much-needed relief from mourning and family responsibilities.

HOW TO USE THIS BOOK

Grief isn't a linear process, and neither is this book. You may find yourself flipping around from late chapters to earlier ones based on your child's needs. Each chapter's activities are organized by the age group the exercise is best suited for, from youngest to oldest.

If you're unsure of where to begin, Chapter 3: Helping Kids Learn about Grief, is a good place to start. From there, children may need help coping with the strong emotions that come with grief. You can find suggestions for coping skills and ways to express feelings of anger, sadness, and anxiety in Chapters 4, 5, 6, and 7.

The later chapters of this book help children speak more directly about their grief, make sense of their experiences, and cultivate hope for the future. It may make sense to turn to these chapters after children have had a chance to learn the earlier emotion-regulation skills. Some children may benefit from going back and forth between telling their story and processing the emotions the stories bring up.

Each activity offers information about what age the exercise is best suited for and the number of children needed to play it. These are suggestions, rather than a hard-and-fast rule: most activities don't require an exact number of children, though they will work best with no more than six players; whether it's best played indoors, out-doors, and/or online; the materials you'll need; and a list of common childhood skills your child will employ while doing the activity. For example, common skills include:

★ **Creativity:** Kids of all ages can use creative outlets like drawing or crafting to help express feelings that may be too big, difficult, or abstract to put into words.

*   **Communication:** Children who are able to speak openly about their grief tend to cope better than those who push down their feelings. Activities that encourage sharing positive and negative thoughts and feelings keep lines of communication open, and strengthen the bond between children and caregivers.
*   **Emotional intelligence:** Children who can't put their feelings into words are more likely to express their emotions through their behavior. We can help children identify and name feelings in order to deepen their understanding of grief.
*   **Emotional regulation:** Strong feelings such as anger, sadness, and fear are normal and common after grief. Learning coping skills and positive outlets for strong feelings allows children to work through their grief in a healthy way.
*   **Relaxation:** After a highly stressful event, children may find themselves feeling anxious or on edge. Relaxation skills help children learn to self-soothe and regain a sense of safety after loss.
*   **Mindfulness:** Focusing on what's happening at the present moment can help children find a sense of calm and manage difficult memories or fears of the future.

You'll then find an explanation of what you or the child needs to know before you start; step-by-step instructions for the exercise itself; and follow-up questions you can ask your child to emphasize points, offer space for concerns, and celebrate progress.

WHEN SHOULD WE START?

Most of this book's activities are not intended for the days and weeks immediately following a death, when children are often in a state of shock. Some signs of shock include:

*   Feeling numb
*   Acting or feeling as though the death didn't really happen
*   Imagining seeing a loved one in public

It may take days, weeks, or even months for shock to subside and other feelings to emerge. When this happens, many children will be more able to speak directly about their grief and make use of this book. Some Chapter 3 activities may be helpful right away, but the rest can wait until after your child has reestablished their routines. Your child may show they are ready by directly talking about the death, asking more questions, or talking or playing about what happened. You might also notice more strong emotions coming to the surface, such as anger or anxiety.

Take your child's lead when introducing activities. Talking about the death reminds your child that grief is not a taboo subject. However, if your child is hesitant, don't force it. Children grieve at their own pace and know when they've had enough. You can try again another day.

You should feel proud about looking out for yourself and your child during such a difficult time. I hope these activities help you and your child as you move forward.

2

ACTIVITIES

In this part, you'll find one hundred activities you can use to help your child navigate grief and loss. Inspired by the stages of grief and tasks of mourning we discussed in Chapter 1, you'll find suggestions to assist your child in doing the difficult emotional work that will help them move through their grieving process and begin to heal.

Each activity has guidelines to help you get started, including the recommended age range, how many children the activity accommodates, what materials you'll need, and where the activity works best. You'll find activities for individuals and groups, indoor and outdoor play, and options if you and your child will be meeting online rather than in person.

We'll start in Chapter 3 by helping your child develop an age-appropriate understanding of death and the grief process. Chapters 4–7 focus on feelings, broadening your child's emotional vocabulary. You'll find creative ways to safely let feelings out, as well as coping skills your child can use when emotions become overwhelming.

Chapters 8 and 9 are an opportunity for your child to speak directly about their experience with grief and their relationship with their loved one. In Chapters 10 and 11, we'll look at grief from a variety of perspectives, including philosophical and spiritual ones, to help your child develop their own personal sense of meaning.

The ages recommended for activities are a suggestion, not a rule. Use your own judgment to decide what feels best for your child based on their interests and maturity level. You are also welcome to move through these chapters in whatever way is most helpful; try them in any order you'd like. If you're unsure of where to begin, Chapter 3 provides activities that help children understand grief, which will help them get the most out of later chapters.

HELPING KIDS LEARN ABOUT GRIEF

In Part 1, you learned about grief and how children of different ages respond to loss. In this chapter, you'll find ways to pass on that grief education to your child in age-appropriate ways. Children need to understand what has happened before they start to process their feelings about loss, so a good understanding of death is crucial before moving on to later chapters.

This chapter offers activities that educate children about death in a variety of ways. Some are fact-based and concrete to help children grasp the concept of death, while others use metaphor to help deepen their understanding of how death makes them feel. There are suggestions for stories and picture books to help children feel less alone in their feelings of grief.

When children are missing information about the death of their loved one, they will mentally "fill in the blanks" with their own assumptions. Often, these assumptions are scarier and more upsetting than what actually occurred. It's common for children to blame themselves for the death, or fear that they or others might die just like their loved one did. Through this chapter's activities, you can help your child get the knowledge they need to alleviate any misplaced guilt or worry.

READ A GRIEF STORY

Consider opening your first conversation about grief and death by reading a book with your child. Stories help children understand that what is happening to them has happened to other people too, and their feelings about it are normal and okay. Cuddle up in person or read together online for an inviting, child-friendly way to explore loss.

Age Range:	**5–7**
Skills:	**Listening, reading comprehension, relaxation**
Materials:	**Children's books on grief, death, and dying; Zoom or another video platform (if playing online)**
Number of Children:	**1+**
Where to Play:	**Inside, online**

BEFORE YOU START
★ Read any books before sharing them with your child or children. Some books refer to belief systems that are different than your child's, or could contain material that is triggering based on your child's specific experiences.
★ Try to anticipate questions your child may bring up so you have time to formulate thoughtful answers.

HOW TO PLAY
★ Find a quiet, mellow time to read. It's okay to be transparent and say you would like to read a book that talks about what happens when a loved one dies.
★ Offer your child some control over the experience by providing several books they can choose from. For younger children (under age seven), find a simple story that speaks about death in straightforward terms. Some good choices include:
  • *Goodbye Mousie* by Robie H. Harris
  • *I Miss You* by Pat Thomas
  • *The Dead Bird* by Margaret Wise Brown
  • *Ida, Always* by Caron Levis and Charles Santoso
★ Older children (seven and up) may be ready to speak more directly about causes of death, or talk about death using metaphors. For these children, consider:
  • *When Dinosaurs Die* by Laurie Krasny Brown and Marc Brown
  • *Tear Soup* by Chuck DeKlyen and Pat Schwiebert
  • *The Fall of Freddie the Leaf* by Leo Buscaglia*

(continued on next page)

* Read the book to your child, taking time to digest the words as well as to take a close look at the illustrations together.
* Pause when needed to answer questions as they come up. You can also ask your child comprehension questions such as "What do you think happened on this page?" or "How does this character feel?" if it feels appropriate to do so.

*Note: This book makes one reference to death being like falling asleep. To avoid confusion, leave out this line when reading to younger children who are still developing their understanding of death.

REFLECTION AND LEARNING QUESTIONS
* What were some of the feelings the main character felt?
* Why did the character feel that way?
* Who or what was around to help the character in this story when they were grieving?
* Did anybody do anything in this book that helped them remember a special person who died?
* Do you have any questions for me about this book?

Children may be more likely to talk about the experiences of a make-believe character because it's less overwhelming than speaking about their own loss, but sometimes it may still be too hard. It's okay if your child refuses a book the first time you offer. Follow their lead, and try again another day.

5 WS ABOUT DEATH

It's not uncommon for young children to ask repeated questions about a loved one's death as a way of processing the event. The 5 Ws are a familiar structure for early elementary school–aged children, and they can help kids to organize and review information.

Age Range:	**5–7**
Skills:	**Listening**
Materials:	**Paper, markers**
Number of Children:	**1**
Where to Play:	**Inside**

BEFORE YOU START

★ Review the 5 Ws with your child: Who, When, Where, What, and Why.

HOW TO PLAY

★ Using five markers of different colors, write five Ws down the left-hand margin of the page, leaving room for writing in between each W.

★ Using the first W as your starting point, write "Who Died?" Answer the question using your child's chosen name for their loved one. For example, Auntie Jen, Poppa, or Sam. Read everything aloud if your child is still learning to read.

★ Moving on to the second W, write "When Did He/She Die?" Answer with as much specificity as you can as far as time of day or day of the week.

★ For the third W, write "Where Did He/She Die?" Be simple and specific, such as "at Grandma's house" or "in the hospital."

★ For the fourth W, write "What Happened?" Provide a simple, one-sentence explanation, such as "Auntie Jen had lung cancer" or "Poppa had a heart attack."

★ For the fifth W, write "Why Did It Happen?" Explain in child-friendly terms what physically stopped working in the body. For example, "Poppa's had a problem with his heart and it stopped working right. His heart stopped beating, and that made his body die." If you're unsure of the cause of death, it's okay to say something like "We aren't sure what happened yet. We can guess that something very sudden happened to Auntie Jen that made her body get very sick and stop working."

REFLECTION AND LEARNING QUESTIONS

★ Is there anything about your special person's death you aren't sure about?

★ How are you feeling after talking about this?

TOY FUNERAL

Children lack the frame of reference to understand funeral rituals the way adults do. The same mourning activities that are comforting or familiar to us may be upsetting to a child. You can use play to help your child better understand what to expect at a funeral before attending together.

Age Range:	**5–7**
Skills:	**Listening, self-reflection, communication**
Materials:	**Small dolls or figurines, small box**
Number of Children:	**1**
Where to Play:	**Inside**

BEFORE YOU START

★ Books can be a great conversation starter when talking to a child about funerals. *When Dinosaurs Die* by Laurie Krasny Brown and Marc Brown and *The Endless Story* by Melissa Kircher are two options that discuss funerals as well as how other cultures mourn their dead.

HOW TO PLAY

★ If you are preparing for a loved one's funeral or memorial service, tell your child about it. Let them know that soon there will be an event happening for your special person. You can explain that this ritual is a special time when many people who knew and loved the person who died come together to remember them, show respect, and say goodbye.

★ Talk about when and where the event will be held. Describe what the location will look like, who will attend, and whether there will be a casket or urn present.

★ Use your dolls or small toys to explore how the event might look and feel. Set up your dolls and any other available props to show your child how everything might look at the event. Show where people will sit and where the casket, urn, or other important items will be. If there will be a casket present, you can use a small box as a stand-in to show what this will look like. You can place a doll inside.

★ If the body will be visible, talk about what the dead body will look like. Prepare children for the ways in which dead bodies are different than living people. For example, your loved one's eyes will be closed, they may look a little different than we remember them, and their skin will be cool to the touch.

* Walk your child through any rituals they may experience, such as singing hymns, listening to friends or family talk about the deceased person, or walking up to the casket to say goodbye. You can play these out with your toys or dolls.
* Play out how others might behave or react, for example, by crying, hugging, sharing gifts, or even telling stories and laughing. Remind your child that any of these feelings are normal when someone dies.
* Help your child anticipate what will happen after the ceremony is over by acting out what happens next, such as returning home, traveling to a grave site, or sharing a meal.
* If necessary, remind your child that a dead person cannot think or feel, so it will not scare them or hurt them to be in a casket, buried, or cremated.

REFLECTION AND LEARNING QUESTIONS

* Is there anything about the event you're still curious or not sure about?
* How do you feel about possibly going to the event?
* Can you think of anything special that you would like to do at home to honor our loved one?
* Is there a way that you would like to participate if you choose to go?

LIFE-CYCLE DRAWING

All living things are born, grow up, age, and eventually die. This art activity helps children to understand that death is a part of life for all living things, including human beings. Learning about the life cycle sets a good foundation for further exploration about death and grieving.

Age Range:	**5–8**
Skills:	**Creativity**
Materials:	**Paper plate, markers or colored pencils**
Number of Children:	**1**
Where to Play:	**Inside**

BEFORE YOU START
★ I highly recommend reading *Lifetimes: The Beautiful Way to Explain Death to Children* by Bryan Mellonie and Robert Ingpen before starting this activity, especially for nature-loving children. Its detailed animal illustrations show how many different species follow the same life cycle of birth, growth, and death.

HOW TO PLAY
★ Review the stages of the life cycle with your child. You can say something such as:

Did you know all living things have a life cycle? Every animal is born a baby, grows up, becomes an adult, and eventually dies. Plants have a life cycle too. They begin as seeds, sprout into seedlings, grow up, and then wither away when their time is done.

★ Ask your child to pick a plant or animal to illustrate for this activity. Any plant or animal can work, but species that have very clear life-cycle stages—birds, frogs, and butterflies, for example—work especially well for this activity.
★ Research your child's chosen plant or animal online to learn more about it. You can run image searches to find pictures of how this plant or animal appears in different stages of life.
★ Divide your paper plate into four sections by drawing two perpendicular lines. Label the top-right section as "Birth," the bottom-right section as "Young," the bottom left as "Grown up," and the top left as "Old."

* Have your child draw their chosen plant or animal on the plate as it appears in each of the four life stages.
* When your child's drawing is finished, ask them to share it with you. Your child can tell you any facts they have learned about their plant or animal, and what makes it unique. Ask your child to talk to you about each of the four life stages and what happens to the animal or plant as it grows through its life cycle.

REFLECTION AND LEARNING QUESTIONS

* How does your plant or animal start its life? Does it hatch from an egg, grow from a seed, or is it born as a baby?
* What happens as your plant or animal grows up? How does its body change?
* Does this plant/animal have a short, medium, or long life?
* What are some signs that your plant or animal is getting old or close to the end of its life?
* At the end of the life cycle, this plant/animal dies. What does that mean?
* Can you think of something special or interesting about each stage of the life cycle?

Not all deaths happen in old age. If your loved one died young, explore this concept through additional questions such as "Sometimes, living things die before they reach the end of their life cycle. Can you think of some reasons why that happens?" You can also reflect on the value and uniqueness of every life, no matter how long or short.

TRUE OR FALSE TOSS

When children have gaps in their knowledge about death, they tend to fill in those blanks with assumptions that can lead to further guilt and worry. This activity dispels possible misconceptions and provides age-appropriate information, using a fun format that can make talking about heavy subjects a little easier.

Age Range:	5–8
Skills:	Listening
Materials:	Ball; two buckets, boxes, or trash cans
Number of Children:	1+
Where to Play:	Inside, outside

BEFORE YOU START
★ Review the following list of prompts on your own, and add any additional true/false statements you feel would be helpful based on your children's individual circumstances.

HOW TO PLAY
★ Find an indoor or outdoor location with enough space to throw a ball.
★ Set up your two buckets or other containers on one side of the room or yard. Select one bucket to be the "true" bucket and the other to be the "false" bucket.
★ Tell your children you will be reading a sentence that has to do with death. Their job is to throw the ball into the "true" bucket if they think the statement is true, and into the "false" bucket if they think it is not.
★ Read the following prompts to your children, and have them take turns tossing the ball to determine whether the statement is true or false:
  • Death is permanent. When a person dies, they cannot come back.
  • People die when their bodies stop working because they are too old, sick, or hurt.
  • Thinking mean thoughts about a person can cause them to die.
  • When a person dies, they can't think, feel, breathe, move, or eat anymore.
  • Misbehaving or being bad can cause a person to die.
  • It's normal to have a hard time believing somebody you love has died.
  • Death isn't contagious, and you can't catch it from being near someone who died.
  • Getting into a serious accident can cause somebody to die.

- It's normal to have all kinds of feelings like anger, sadness, and relief after somebody dies.
- All living things die.
- Most people die after they have lived a very long life.
- Sometimes, young people and even babies can die.
- A funeral (or other event your family is conducting) is a special time for people to say goodbye to a loved one who has died.
- Nothing a child says, does, or thinks can make another person get sick or die.
- The thoughts and feelings a person has after somebody dies are called grief.
- It's normal for grief feelings to come and go.
- Even after somebody we love has died, we can still think about them, talk about them, and love them.

★ If a child incorrectly identifies a statement, pause the game. You can ask another child to try answering the question, or gently explain the answer and reasoning behind it yourself.

★ If you identify any serious misunderstandings that could be causing guilt or worry for your child, take the time to explore those more deeply after the game ends.

REFLECTION AND LEARNING QUESTIONS

★ Did you learn anything new about death or grief from playing this game?

★ Have you had any of these feelings or worries yourself?

★ What have you learned about grief or death that is surprising or unexpected?

★ Did this game bring up any other questions for you?

WHERE IS MY LOVED ONE NOW?

For young children, the afterlife is an abstract concept that takes time and repetition to grasp. Older children may have their own thoughts and ideas to share. Inviting children to draw their vision of the afterlife is an opportunity to review your family's beliefs and spot any misunderstandings.

Age Range:	5–11
Skills:	Listening, creativity
Materials:	Paper, art supplies, video platform with whiteboard function (for online play)
Number of Children:	1
Where to Play:	Inside, online

BEFORE YOU START
★ *The Endless Story* by Melissa Kircher looks at death in a gentle, philosophical way and explores how different cultures think about death and the afterlife.

HOW TO PLAY
★ If you didn't begin by reading *The Endless Story*, talk with your child about how people around the world have different ideas about what might happen after we die. If it feels right for your family, you can talk in detail about these ideas, such as heaven, reincarnation, returning to nature, or becoming ancestors.
★ Talk with your child about the basics of your own family's beliefs about what happens after death.
★ Ask your child to draw a picture of where they imagine their loved one is now.
★ Ask your child to explain their picture to you. Keep an eye out for details that indicate a lack of understanding that could cause distress, for example, concerns that a loved one may be cold or afraid because they have been buried.
★ Wrap up your conversation by reviewing the things we do know for sure about death: It's permanent, and when people die their bodies stop feeling, thinking, and moving.

REFLECTION AND LEARNING QUESTIONS
★ How do you feel when you think about the afterlife?
★ Do you think our loved ones watch over us after they die?
★ What is something about the afterlife that you wonder about?

TEAR SOUP

Tear Soup by Chuck DeKlyen and Pat Schwiebert is a quirky book with fairy-tale elements that teaches children about many facets of grief. After reading, help your children create their own "recipe" for the grief process to make the book's lessons more tangible.

Age Range:	**5–11**
Skills:	**Listening, creativity, reading comprehension**
Materials:	**Large bowl, scissors, construction paper, wooden spoon, pens or pencils, sticky notes**
Number of Children:	**1+**
Where to Play:	**Inside**

BEFORE YOU START

★ *Tear Soup* is a fairly long, complex story, so it helps to read it once in advance so children can familiarize themselves with it.

★ Cut out roughly 3-inch teardrop shapes out of various colors of construction paper. Aim for three to five teardrops per player.

HOW TO PLAY

★ Reread *Tear Soup* with your child or children. On this second read-through, ask your children to keep an eye out for any "ingredients" for tear soup that show up in the story.

★ You can help draw your children's attention to any or all of the following aspects of grieving as they arise in the book:

- Crying
- Feeling sad
- Wanting to be alone
- Thinking of memories
- Body pain
- Feeling empty
- Anger
- Confusion
- Feeling tired or heavy
- Feeling mad at God
- Holding on to your loved one's belongings
- Yelling or acting out
- Jealousy
- Not feeling like having fun

★ When you've finished the book, suggest to your children that you create your own special version of tear soup.

(continued on next page)

* Hand out your paper teardrops and ask each child to draw or write down one ingredient on each of their pieces of paper. They can choose examples from the book or invent their own.
* Have children take turns sharing their ingredients and placing them in the bowl.
* Younger children may enjoy stirring the pot; you can have them use the wooden spoon to do this in order to prepare your soup. Ask your children how long they think it will take for your soup to cook. Days? Weeks? Months? Years?
* Help your children to name people and things that can help you while you're making tear soup. Write or draw their ideas on sticky notes, and ask children to stick the notes to the outside of the bowl. If children need prompting, here are some examples from the story:
  * Friends who can listen to you
  * Exercise
  * Yummy comfort food
  * Gratitude
  * Taking breaks
  * Being around other grievers
* For younger children, take turns pretending to taste your finished soup. What does it taste like? For older children, think aloud about which friends or family members might help you by "sharing your soup," the book's metaphor for listening, empathizing with, and supporting a griever.

REFLECTION AND LEARNING QUESTIONS

* Do you think everybody makes tear soup the same way? Why or why not?
* Is there a right or wrong way to grieve?
* Grandy learns that "quicker doesn't always mean better." Why does tear soup take time?
* Sometimes it's hard for people to talk about grief. Why do you think that is?
* What are things that people say or do when a person is grieving that aren't so helpful?

....

This book and activity are a great opportunity to demonstrate for children that grieving doesn't have to happen all at once. Just as Grandy sometimes picks up her soup and sometimes sets it down, children can alternate between grieving intensely and returning to the "normal" playful activities of childhood.

....

TANGLED GRIEF YARN TOSS

Grief is not a neat or tidy process. Even though many people experience stages of grief, they don't always happen in order or progress in a linear way. This group activity shows children that shifting between a range of emotions is a normal and healthy part of working through grief.

Age Range:	5–11
Skills:	Emotional intelligence, self-reflection
Materials:	Ball of yarn, marker, name tag stickers or paper and tape
Number of Children:	4+
Where to Play:	Inside, outside

BEFORE YOU START

★ This activity works best with a larger number of people, so if you have a smaller group of children you should recruit extra adults to play with you.

HOW TO PLAY

★ Find an indoor or outdoor location with lots of space to play.
★ Review the common stages of grief with your participants: Shock, Denial, Bargaining, Guilt, Anger, Depression, and Hope. For younger children or smaller groups, you can shorten the list to include just a few of these.
★ Assign each player one of the seven stages from the list. Use your name stickers or create labels with paper and tape to label each player with their assigned grief stage. Double up if you don't have seven players, but give anyone with more than one stage two stages that are next to each other.
★ Arrange your participants in a circle following the order of the stages of grief as best you can, starting with Shock and ending with Hope.
★ Read or paraphrase the following:

When a person is grieving, they might feel like their feelings are supposed to happen in perfect order. One day we might feel shocked, and then angry, and then sad, and then eventually we start to feel hopeful and never feel those other feelings again. But that's not really how it works. Our feelings can move in all different directions, like a web. Let's see if we can make a web now!

(continued on next page)

* Hand the ball of yarn to the first child in your circle. Ask them to hold on to the free end of the yarn, but have them toss the ball to someone across the circle from them so that the yarn begins to unravel.
* Keep tossing the yarn until every participant has taken at least one turn. You will have created a tangled, weblike shape.
* Ask your children to examine the shape they have made and read the next part of the script:

In real life, our feelings are messy and tangled. One day we might be angry, then sad, and then we might be in shock, and then maybe we feel hopeful for a few days. But then maybe something else happens, and we are right back to feeling angry again. We might even feel two feelings at the same time. We might have good days and bad days, and that doesn't mean anything is wrong. That's just how grief works.

* Talk about what "tangled" grief might look or feel like with your children. You can think about expectations around grieving and compare and contrast them with how grief often looks in real life.

REFLECTION AND LEARNING QUESTIONS
* Which of these feelings do you feel the most?
* Which of these feelings do you feel the least?
* Are there any feelings not included in these stages that you'd add to the list?
* Do you ever feel like people are "supposed" to grieve in a certain way or be done feeling sad after a certain amount of time?
* Are you feeling any of these feelings today?

QUESTION MAILBOX

Guilt or shame can make children hesitant to ask questions about grief. Creating a family "mailbox" where children can write down what's on their mind may help them share their thoughts with a trusted adult. Some younger kids might need a sibling's help writing the question. Be prepared for a variety of questions in your mailbox, and answer as simply and as honestly as you can.

Age Range:	5–11
Skills:	Grief education, identifying misconceptions about grief
Materials:	Small cardboard box, tempera paint, scissors, construction paper, metal brad, sticky notes, writing utensils
Number of Children:	1+
Where to Play:	Inside

BEFORE YOU START

★ Explain that you'll be creating a special box today where kids can put any questions they have about death, grief, or anything else on their minds. Set some ground rules with your children on how to use the mailbox. For example, only a trusted grownup will look in the box, and nobody else has to know who asked the question if the asker doesn't want to share their identity.

HOW TO PLAY

★ Paint and decorate your cardboard box.
★ Cut a mailbox flag shape out of your construction paper in the correct size for your box.
★ Once your paint has dried, attach your flag to the side of the box using the metal brad.
★ Select a public place for your mailbox and leave sticky notes and pens nearby.
★ Check the box once a day for notes. Children can indicate when they've put a note in the box by raising the flag.

REFLECTION AND LEARNING QUESTIONS

★ When somebody puts a question in the box, should we all talk about it together, or should the grownup find a private time to talk to the asker alone?
★ Who should answer the questions that are put in the box?

THE BALL IN THE BOX

Lauren Herschel's metaphor about the "ball in the box," popularized on Twitter, has helped many adults find comfort and understanding during grief. This activity makes the analogy more concrete so younger children can appreciate it too.

Age Range:	**6–8**
Skills:	**Listening, self-reflection**
Materials:	**Shoebox, softball, golf ball, marble**
Number of Children:	**1+**
Where to Play:	**Inside**

BEFORE YOU START

★ If you haven't heard of it before, familiarize yourself with the ball in the box analogy on Twitter or elsewhere before getting started.

HOW TO PLAY

★ If necessary, define grief for your children. Try saying something like "Grief is what we call the feelings we feel after somebody we love dies. People who are grieving might feel really sad, angry, confused, shocked, or guilty when they think about their special person who died."

★ Hold up the softball for your child to see.

★ Tell your child:

When a special person dies, our grief starts out like this ball. It's really big. I want you to imagine that inside this shoebox there's a little button, and every time the ball pushes the button, it reminds us of our special person and gives us grief feelings.

★ Place the softball in the shoebox. Ask your child to turn the box and roll the ball around, noticing how many times the ball hits the side of the box.

★ Tell your child:

When our grief is big, it hits the grief button all the time. Do you feel how much it's bumping around in there? You can really feel how strong it is.

* Remove the softball and hold up the golf ball. Tell your child:

Over time, our grief feelings get a little bit smaller, like this. When it rolls around the box, this ball has a little more room.

* Place the ball in the shoebox and ask your child to move the box again. Tell your child:

You can still tell it's there, but it doesn't feel quite so heavy anymore. It doesn't push the button as much as it used to.

* Hold up the marble. Tell your child:

After a long, long time, our grief starts to look like this tiny marble. It never goes away, but it gets so small that sometimes you might not even notice it is there.

* Place the marble in the shoebox and ask your child to roll the marble around. Tell your child:

When our grief gets small, we can go a long time without anything pushing our button. The ball is small and light, and it gets much easier to carry. But every once in a while, our button will still get pushed, and we'll get our same sad, mad, or confused feelings back again. That's okay. It's always okay to feel sad, even if our special person died a long time ago. But over time, it will get easier to deal with those sad feelings when they happen.

REFLECTION AND LEARNING QUESTIONS
* How big do you think your ball of grief is right now? Is it big, medium, or small?
* Can you think of a time when your grief button got pushed?
* How did you feel when that happened?

IF GRIEF WAS A...

Metaphors are a handy way to express feelings that are difficult to put into words. Help kids tap in to their creative thinking and look at grief from new perspectives with this simple online-friendly activity.

Age Range:	**8–11**
Skills:	**Creativity, imagination**
Materials:	**Zoom or another video platform (if playing online)**
Number of Children:	**2+**
Where to Play:	**Inside, outside, online**

BEFORE YOU START

★ This activity works best when children already have some understanding of grief. Try some of the earlier activities in this chapter before introducing this one.

HOW TO PLAY

★ Take turns with your group of children to complete sentence stems like this aloud: "If grief was a color, it would be..." You could replace the word "color" with animal, season, shape, smell, taste, sound, object, place, texture, or your own ideas.
★ Take turns completing prompts yourself to model the activity for your children.
★ When you've finished, ask children to give their own answers to prompts completed by others.
★ As an alternative, children can create their own sentences for others to finish.

REFLECTION AND LEARNING QUESTIONS

★ What was it like hearing other players describe what grief is like for them?
★ If you were going to draw a picture of grief, what would it look like?
★ If we had played this game in the past, do you think your answers would have been different?
★ If we played this game again in the future, do you think your answers would change?

CHAPTER 4

NAMING AND EXPLORING EMOTIONS

The activities in this chapter are intended to build your child's emotional vocabulary. One reason that children throw tantrums or misbehave when they're feeling upset is that they lack the words to tell us how they're feeling. They don't have a choice but to act it out! When we give children words to use to describe their feelings, we open up new possibilities for expressing themselves.

Emotional education serves another important purpose: It helps children know that all their feelings, no matter how intense or difficult, are normal and okay. This can be really helpful for grieving kids, who may be experiencing some emotions for the first time. Grief responses can be powerful, scary, and even involve feeling opposite emotions at once.

In this chapter, you'll find art- and play-based activities that help your child explore emotions both verbally and nonverbally. They'll learn that no mood lasts forever and that it's normal to feel opposite feelings at the same time. Because sometimes grief emotions show up as feelings in the body, we'll explore how physical sensations can clue us in to what we're feeling. Most importantly, children will know that any feeling—big or small, happy or sad—is okay to name and talk about.

FEELINGS IN MY BODY

If you've ever described yourself as "feeling blue" or having "butterflies in your stomach," you know that we often associate feelings with colors and parts of the body. This art activity helps young children do the same—plus, having your body traced is a nice opportunity for bonding.

Age Range:	**5–8**
Skills:	**Creativity, emotional intelligence**
Materials:	**Butcher paper or wrapping paper, pencil, markers or crayons**
Number of Children:	**1**
Where to Play:	**Inside**

BEFORE YOU START
★ Review common idioms people use to describe feelings: for example, feeling "red with anger," being "green with envy," or even "having ants in your pants." Books like *The Color Monster* by Anna Llenas or *My Many Colored Days* by Dr. Seuss are a great way to bring this concept to life.

HOW TO PLAY
★ Tell your child that you're going to make art together that will help them think about where they feel feelings in their own body.
★ Ask your child to carefully lie down on their back on the butcher paper or wrapping paper. The paper should be long enough to fit your child's entire body.
★ Use the pencil to gently trace the outline of your child's body. Once you've finished, your child can get up and help you fill in any breaks in the outline. Your child can add features to their outline, such as a face and hair, to make it more closely resemble them. Leave most of the body as blank space.
★ Ask your child to select a colored marker or crayon to represent each of the following feelings: happy, mad, sad, and afraid. Older children may also wish to include more complex feelings like surprise and disgust.
★ Make a key somewhere on the outside edge of your paper to remind you which color goes with which feeling.

- Discuss how sometimes, our biggest clue that we are having a feeling comes from our body. Feelings can give us headaches or tummy aches, they can make our heart beat quickly, cause our palms to sweat, or make us feel tired or energetic.
- Invite your child to color in their outline to show where they feel each feeling in their body. Your child can do this abstractly using colors, shapes, and lines, or they can pick out symbols that represent how the emotion feels from their point of view.
- Once your child has finished, ask them to tell you about their drawing.

REFLECTION AND LEARNING QUESTIONS
- How did you decide which color to choose for each feeling?
- How can you tell when you are feeling happy, sad, mad, or scared?
- What happens in your body when you feel each of these emotions?
- Have you ever had a feeling that gave you pain in your body?
- Have you ever had a feeling that made you tired or energetic?
- Sometimes when people are grieving, their grief comes out as feelings in their body. Do you think that's ever happened to you? If so, what body feelings have you had?

....

For a variation on this exercise, use a set of scented markers that includes both good and yucky smells, like Crayola Silly Scents. Ask your child to pick a scent they think matches each feeling.

....

SHORT-FILM CRITIC

This activity uses short films to help young kids talk about feelings during virtual play. Caregivers can use these stories as a jumping-off point to help children identify emotions, build empathy, and put feelings into words.

Age Range:	**5–8**
Skills:	**Emotional intelligence, communication**
Materials:	**YouTube, Zoom or another video platform (if playing online)**
Number of Children:	**1+**
Where to Play:	**Inside, online**

BEFORE YOU START
★ Select a short film or two to watch together. Preview your choices in advance so you have an idea of the content.

HOW TO PLAY
★ If you're searching for age-appropriate short films, YouTube is a great resource for free content. You can also check Disney+, which has a wealth of Pixar shorts available to stream that are a great fit for this activity. Here are a few recommendations: *Taking Flight* by Radio Flyer and Moonbot Studios; *Float* by Pixar; *Hair Love* by Sony Pictures Animation (note: this short film includes a character receiving chemotherapy for cancer); *Lava* by Pixar; or *Piper* by Pixar.
★ Watch the video alongside your child or children. If you'd like, pause the movie at key moments to ask questions about how the characters in the film are feeling. Highlight nonverbal communication by asking questions about the characters' tone of voice, body language, and facial expression.
★ After the short is over, encourage your child to put themselves in the shoes of the film's characters and imagine how it would feel to be in that situation.

REFLECTION AND LEARNING QUESTIONS
★ How would you feel if someone treated you this way?
★ How do you think this character was feeling during this part of the movie? How could you tell?
★ What does this character's body tell us about how they are feeling?
★ If this happened to you, what would you do?

DOUBLE-DIP FEELINGS GRAB BAG

Conflicting, contradictory feelings are a natural part of grief. However, they can be troubling for children, who tend to think only in black and white. The book *Double-Dip Feelings* by Barbara S. Cain and Anne Patterson, along with the following activity, can help children explore what it means to feel two things at once.

Age Range:	**5–8**
Skills:	**Emotional intelligence**
Materials:	**Pen, paper, scissors, bowl or hat**
Number of Children:	**2+**
Where to Play:	**Inside**

BEFORE YOU START
★ Read the book *Double-Dip Feelings* with your children.

HOW TO PLAY
★ Write down the following feeling words on separate strips of paper:

- Angry
- Sad
- Happy
- Scared
- Excited
- Nervous
- Embarrassed
- Jealous
- Silly
- Frustrated
- Grateful
- Tired
- Playful
- Guilty
- Brave
- Shy
- Mean
- Friendly

★ Place your strips in the bowl or hat and mix them up.
★ Take turns pulling two strips from the bowl. Ask your children to try to imagine a time when a person might feel both those feelings at the same time.
★ Older children can assist younger ones if they pull a difficult pair. Similarly, you can use your turns to model how to play and provide examples of your own.
★ Continue playing until you've pulled all strips or until interest wanes.

REFLECTION AND LEARNING QUESTIONS
★ Which feeling pairs were easiest? Which were hardest?
★ Can you think of a time when a person might feel three feelings at once?
★ After someone dies, it's normal to feel opposite feelings at the same time. Can you think of a time when you've felt that way?

YOU CAN'T PUSH DOWN FEELINGS

Some children hope that by avoiding talking about their negative emotions, they can make them go away. This exercise shows children why it helps to share feelings, rather than push them down.

Age Range:	**5–8**
Skills:	**Emotional intelligence**
Materials:	**Beach ball or Ping-Pong ball**
Number of Children:	**1**
Where to Play:	**Inside or outside**

BEFORE YOU START

★ Tell your child: "After somebody dies, we can have lots of emotions that don't feel good, like sadness or anger. Because they don't feel good, they might be hard to talk about. Sometimes, people decide they don't want to share those bad feelings at all. They hope that if they don't, maybe the feelings will just disappear. This activity will help us understand why that doesn't work."

HOW TO PLAY

★ If playing outside, ask your child to submerge the beach ball under water in a pool or inflatable pool. If playing inside, fill a sink or tub with water and have the child press the Ping-Pong ball under the surface.

★ Read to your child:

Instead of letting feelings out, a person might try to push them back down instead, just like you're pushing on that ball. Do you feel what is happening? Is the ball sinking down to the bottom? Nope! If you pay attention, you might feel that it's trying to push back up. The harder you push down, the harder the ball pushes up. No matter how hard you push, the ball is going to pop back up again. Your feelings do the same thing. If you try to push them down, they'll just pop back up again. Feelings need to come out.

REFLECTION AND LEARNING QUESTIONS

★ What are some ways you can let feelings out?

★ What do you think it looks or feels like when someone's pushed-down feelings pop up?

★ Who can you talk to if you are having hard feelings like anger or sadness?

FEELINGS CHARADES

This classic party game has a hidden benefit: It's great for helping kids learn about how emotions are expressed through facial expressions and body language. It's also easy to adapt for virtual play.

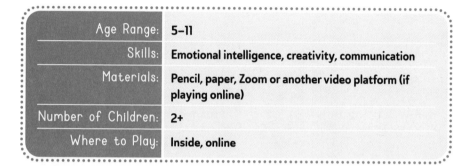

Age Range:	**5–11**
Skills:	**Emotional intelligence, creativity, communication**
Materials:	**Pencil, paper, Zoom or another video platform (if playing online)**
Number of Children:	**2+**
Where to Play:	**Inside, online**

BEFORE YOU START

★ If you're playing online, ensure all players are seated far away enough from their cameras that their bodies are visible.

★ Review the rules of charades with any players who aren't familiar with the game.

HOW TO PLAY

★ If playing in person, write a list of feelings words on your paper and tear it into strips. If playing online, feelings can be sent to players via private message, or players may choose their own. (Sample feelings include angry, sad, happy, scared, nervous, excited, embarrassed, silly, tired, brave, and frustrated.)

★ Have children take turns acting out their assigned or selected feelings without speaking or making sounds and continue until another player guesses correctly.

★ Continue the game for as many rounds as you like.

REFLECTION AND LEARNING QUESTIONS

★ What were the easiest and hardest feelings to guess?

★ Which feelings were most fun to act out? Why?

★ Have you ever noticed how someone was feeling without them having to tell you? How could you tell what they were feeling?

If you'd like to mix things up, players can work together in pairs to act out their chosen emotion. Alternatively, one child can try to convey two feelings at once, similar to the Double-Dip Feelings Grab Bag activity in this chapter.

GRIEF JENGA

Kids often struggle to answer open-ended questions about their thoughts and feelings. Game play makes sharing feel less intimidating, and it provides extra structure to help kids delve deeper into their thoughts, questions, and worries.

Age Range:	**5–11**
Skills:	**Emotional intelligence, communication**
Materials:	**Jenga or block tower game, markers or stickers, pen, paper**
Number of Children:	**1+**
Where to Play:	**Inside**

BEFORE YOU START

★ Prep your blocks in advance so you're ready to play. Divide the blocks into even groups. Most games have fifty-four blocks, so you can create six groups of nine blocks. Use a marker or sticker to color-code your blocks with a large dot in the center of each one that is visible only when the block is pulled out of the tower. Choose six colors that offer variety and are easy to distinguish from each other, but let your child decide which color to associate with each prompt.

★ You can also think of responses to share on your turns in the game. Sharing age-appropriate positive and negative feelings with your child or children will make it easier for them to share too.

HOW TO PLAY

★ If your children have never played Jenga before, review the rules before starting the game: Players take turns drawing a block from the tower, and they try to keep the tower standing as long as possible.

★ Tell your child that in this version of the game, each time a player draws a block, they'll also share something about themselves from a category that matches their block color. Let your child know that all players have the choice to "pass" if they don't feel comfortable sharing something about the category they pull.

★ Take turns with your child assigning a prompt to each block category, and then write down the choices on your paper. Ideally, there should be a mix of positive and negative feelings and shallow and deep questions. Not all prompts need to be grief-related. You can use the following prompts for inspiration or create your own:

- Sometimes I wonder about...
- A happy memory of my loved one is...
- A sad memory of my loved one is...
- A funny memory of my loved one is...
- I feel angry when...
- If I had three wishes, I would...
- I feel scared when...
- I think it's unfair that...
- I wish I could change...
- Something I love is...

★ The youngest player goes first. Take turns with your children pulling one block each from the tower, trying not to make the tower fall.

★ Answer the prompt that corresponds with your block color.

★ This game is a great opportunity to normalize your child's feelings. As they are sharing on their turns, take the opportunity to let them know that their feelings are valid. A quick comment like "I get why you'd feel that way" or "I bet many kids think that when someone dies" can go a long way.

★ Once the tower falls, the game is done! You can put it away for another day or play again with new prompts.

REFLECTION AND LEARNING QUESTIONS

★ How was this game for you? Was it easy or hard?

★ Which was your favorite color to get?

★ Which was your least favorite color to get?

★ Did any of my answers surprise you?

Sometimes. games like this reveal inaccurate beliefs about a loved one's death that are causing unnecessary worry or guilt. If you pick up on this. you can pause the game to discuss or make sure to follow up after. Activities in Chapter 3 can help clear up misunderstandings.

DRAWING TO MUSIC

We all know what it's like to have an emotional response to music. Drawing or painting to a variety of songs is a great way to explore how different music makes us feel, and how feelings influence our behavior. This activity works in person or virtually with some adaptation.

Age Range:	**5–11**
Skills:	**Emotional intelligence, creativity**
Materials:	**Paper; crayons, colored pencils, or paint; Zoom or another video platform (if playing online)**
Number of Children:	**1+**
Where to Play:	**Inside, online**

BEFORE YOU START

★ Compile a playlist of songs on your phone or computer. Include music from a wide variety of genres that evoke different emotions. Consider classical music, sad or suspenseful movie soundtracks, hard rock or heavy metal, Disney songs, upbeat pop music, percussion, and lullabies.

HOW TO PLAY

★ Tell the child or children that you'll be making art today while listening to music. Encourage them to notice how the music makes them feel and have them draw or paint those feelings on their paper.

★ If you're in person, play brief (thirty- to sixty-second) clips of the songs from your playlist. If online, share your screen to play music directly from your computer.

★ With each music change, instruct your child to get a fresh piece of paper and make a new drawing or painting. Offer a few reminders to bring their attention back to the music if it wanders.

★ Share your completed drawings with each other.

★ For an added challenge, see if other players can guess which art goes with which song.

REFLECTION AND LEARNING QUESTIONS

★ Which of the songs was your favorite, and why?

★ How are the art pieces for each song similar? How are they different?

★ Do you think music can help us change how we feel?

FEELINGS CHANGE LIKE THE WEATHER

This activity helps children learn that no feeling, no matter how intense, lasts forever. Imagining emotional states as types of weather provides an opportunity for expressing feelings nonverbally, which can help children share deeper emotions that might be hard to put into words.

Age Range:	**6–9**
Skills:	**Emotional intelligence, creativity**
Materials:	**Paper, art materials, video platform with whiteboard function (for online play)**
Number of Children:	**1+**
Where to Play:	**Inside, online**

BEFORE YOU START

★ Invite your children to name as many states of weather as they can think of: rain, snow, sun, hail, wind, fog, tornadoes, hurricanes, etc. Ask your children how these different types of weather make them feel. Tell your children that today you'll think about how our feelings can sometimes be like weather.

HOW TO PLAY

★ Tell your children:

Think about all the different kinds of weather you've experienced in your life. No weather lasts forever, because the world around us is always changing. Even the biggest storm eventually passes through, and some new kind of weather follows behind it. Your feelings are the same way. When you're in the middle of a big emotion, it might feel like it's going to be that way forever. But just like the weather, your feelings come and go.

★ Ask each child to choose a feeling to illustrate. If this feeling were a type of weather, what would it look like?
★ Have each child share their finished drawing with the group, without naming the feeling they illustrated. Take turns trying to guess the feeling represented by each drawing.

(continued on next page)

* Ask each child to draw another weather picture on the reverse side of their paper that represents how they are feeling today.
* Share these second drawings with the group.

REFLECTION AND LEARNING QUESTIONS

* We can't change the weather, but do you think it's ever possible to change your feelings? Why or why not?
* What clues did you look for in other people's pictures to guess what feeling they were drawing?
* Have you ever had a feeling that felt like it would never go away?

JOINT STORYTELLING

Storytelling allows children to express feelings and experiences from a safe distance. Talking about someone else's made-up experience is less threatening than telling a story about yourself, but it still provides opportunities for exploration. This works well as a virtual play activity.

Age Range:	**8–11**
Skills:	**Emotional intelligence, creativity, communication**
Materials:	**Pen and paper or phone, Zoom or another video platform (if playing online)**
Number of Children:	**1+**
Where to Play:	**Inside, online**

BEFORE YOU START

★ Explain that today, you'll be telling a story together. You'll do it by taking turns, adding one sentence at a time, until the story is done. The story can be about anything.

HOW TO PLAY

★ Choose how you'd like to tell your story. If playing online, offer to take turns writing the story in the chat box—kids often find this very fun. If playing in person, you can give the option of writing the story down or using your phone to record it.
★ Identify who would like to start the story. If playing in a group, the honor may go to the youngest player. If one-on-one, let the child choose who should begin.
★ It's often easiest to start the story with a simple "Once upon a time..." sentence.
★ Take turns adding on to the story until you find a satisfying ending. If you sense the story is going on too long and players are losing interest, feel free to move the plot along by asking players how they think the story should end.

REFLECTION AND LEARNING QUESTIONS

★ Do you think there was a moral to this story?
★ Who do you think was the hero of the story?
★ Was there a villain?
★ Which character was most like you?

FEELINGS MASK

Sometimes, children bottle up negative feelings after loss. This may be especially true for tweens, for whom friendships with peers are increasingly important. This art activity helps older kids explore how their inner thoughts and feelings may differ from the "mask" they wear in front of others.

Age Range:	**9–11**
Skills:	**Emotional intelligence, creativity**
Materials:	**Paper mask, paint, assorted craft materials (sequins, magazine cutouts, feathers, gems, etc.)**
Number of Children:	**1**
Where to Play:	**Inside**

BEFORE YOU START
* Prep your materials. Blank full-face paper masks can be purchased online from retailers like Amazon or Michaels, or you can look online to find an outline you can trace.

HOW TO PLAY
* Tell your child you'd like to try an art project today that can help them talk about themselves and their feelings.
* Talk with your child about what it means to "put on a mask" or to "mask one's feelings" in public. Let your child know that it's normal to mask our feelings sometimes in order to get through the day.
* Think out loud with your child about how the "mask" they wear changes in different settings. For example, your child may act differently when at school compared to hanging out with friends at home.
* Using paint and any craft items you have on hand, ask your child to decorate the outward-facing side of the mask. This side will represent how your child is perceived by other people.
* Ask your child to decorate the inner-facing part of the mask to represent how they see themselves.
* Once the mask is complete, ask your child to share their finished design with you. Try to avoid interpreting the meaning yourself—instead, focus your comments on the choices your child made in their art and ask them questions.

REFLECTION AND LEARNING QUESTIONS

* How was this art project for you?
* How do you feel about how other people see you?
* Do you think the way other people see you is accurate?
* Is there anything from inside your mask that you wish other people could see?

FEELINGS COLOR MAP

This simple art activity helps older kids label feelings and express them by assigning them a color, shape, and size. The map can be a helpful metaphor for navigating feelings, just like explorers navigate uncharted territory. Because it requires very few materials, it works equally well virtually and in person.

Age Range:	10–11
Skills:	Emotional intelligence, creativity
Materials:	Paper, markers or colored pencils, Zoom or another video platform (if playing online)
Number of Children:	1
Where to Play:	Inside, online

BEFORE YOU START

★ If you're playing virtually, make sure both you and your child have the needed supplies in each of your locations.

HOW TO PLAY

★ If your child needs some context before getting started, introduce this activity by saying something like:

I'd like us to create maps of our emotions. A map of a city tells us about all the important places we will find there and gives us an idea of how big or small things are. Many maps use something called a key to let us know what different symbols represent. For these feelings maps, we're going to pick different colors to represent each feeling we might have had today. You can create a key in the corner of your paper so we remember which color goes with which feeling.

★ Help your child to identify emotions they have felt today and select a color for each one. If your child is having trouble coming up with multiple emotions, broaden the time frame to include all feelings experienced in the past week.
★ Assign a color to each emotion. Your child can create a key in the upper corner of their map as a reminder of what color corresponds with which emotion.
★ Your child can create their map by drawing a shape to represent each feeling. The size of the shape shows whether the feeling was felt in a big, medium, or small amount. The shape and color can give us information about what the emotion felt like. Anger might be spiky and red, or sadness could be gray and droopy.

★ Create your own map alongside your child to use as a model. You can give your child permission to share negative feelings by sharing some of your own. For example, consider making statements such as:

I was really stressed out this morning about having enough time to pack for our trip. I'm going to choose gray to represent worry and draw a big cloud shape all over the top of my paper. I also got a tiny bit annoyed at our neighbor, so I'm going to pick red and put down a few teeny little dots to show that I was just a little bit mad.

★ After you and your child have both completed your maps, take turns sharing them with each other. Describe when you felt each of the emotions you illustrated on your map. You can also explain why you chose to depict each emotion the way that you did.

★ You can revisit this activity periodically to check in with your child about their current feelings. This gets children into the habit of being in touch with their emotions and helps them notice how seemingly large and overpowering feelings can change over time.

REFLECTION AND LEARNING QUESTIONS

★ What was the biggest feeling on your map? What was the smallest?
★ Are there any opposite emotions on your map?
★ How would this map have been different if we'd drawn it yesterday or last month?
★ How do you think your map might look tomorrow?
★ Is there anything you wish you could change about your map?

CHAPTER 5

COPING WITH WORRIES

A loved one's death makes the world feel less safe for children. Threats and dangers that used to seem abstract suddenly feel more real. Routines are out of order, and nothing feels the same as it used to. And, most importantly, someone your child loved and relied on is no longer here to comfort them.

It's common for kids to experience anxiety after a death. The disruption to the usual flow of daily life can make children feel less secure, and they may cling to caregivers as a way to protect themselves. Children may become more aware of mortality in general, which can lead to heightened worries about health and safety. You may hear your child asking about their own death or the possibility that something could happen to you.

In this chapter, you'll find many tools your child can use to soothe anxiety. Relaxation skills help to calm the body and mind, while thought-based activities help children notice unhelpful thinking patterns that may cause them to worry more than they need to. Finally, children will have opportunities to voice their fears about death, which will deepen their understanding of anxiety and the role it plays in their grief.

FLOWER BREATHING

Having a prop for breathing exercises provides young children with a focus for the activity, making it easier to complete. Pipe-cleaner flowers are fun for children to make, and they lend themselves to pretend play involving deep, slow breathing.

Age Range:	**5–7**
Skills:	**Relaxation, emotional regulation**
Materials:	**Several pipe cleaners per participant**
Number of Children:	**1+**
Where to Play:	**Inside**

BEFORE YOU START

★ Talk with your child or children about how taking deep breaths can help to relax our bodies and brains when we're feeling worried.

HOW TO PLAY

★ Tell your children that you'll be creating their favorite flower out of pipe cleaners, then doing a breathing exercise with it. Create a flower for yourself too, so you can demonstrate the deep-breathing technique.
★ Start with a single green pipe cleaner for a stem, then twist other colors around it to add petals and leaves.
★ Show your child how to pretend to smell their flower by taking a deep breath in through the nose. Encourage your children to really imagine what the flower would smell like.
★ Now slowly blow your breath out onto the flower to show your child how to make the flower sway in the breeze when you exhale.
★ Guide your child as they practice inhaling and exhaling on their own.

REFLECTION AND LEARNING QUESTIONS

★ Was it easy, medium, or hard to try flower breathing?
★ How is this breathing different from your normal breath?
★ Did you notice any difference in how you felt after taking some deep breaths?
★ Can you think of times when it might be helpful to bring your flower along to practice your breathing?

BEANBAG BREATHING

Deep breathing works best when kids are breathing from the diaphragm, deep in the belly. This type of breathing can be tricky to teach because it's not how kids breathe every day. Using a toy helps young kids get the hang of this skill.

Age Range:	**5–8**
Skills:	**Relaxation, emotional regulation**
Materials:	**Small beanbag, toy, or action figure**
Number of Children:	**1**
Where to Play:	**Inside**

BEFORE YOU START
★ Find a comfy, carpeted spot where your child can relax on the floor. Ask your child for help selecting a toy and location to practice. Toys that have a bit of weight to them work best for this activity.

HOW TO PLAY
★ Help your child get settled on the floor, lying on their back. Their feet should be planted firmly on the floor, with their knees bent, pointing up toward the sky. Their arms should be relaxed at their sides.
★ Place your child's chosen toy on their belly and read the following script:

Let's use your breath to take your toy for a ride. Take a deep breath in through your nose and imagine it filling up your belly like a balloon. Keep filling your belly with air and watch your toy rise up in the air! Hello there!

Okay, now the toy wants to come back down again. Let's let the air out through your mouth and slowly deflate your belly so it comes back down again. Keep the ride going, slowly and smoothly. Slowly breathe in, and watch the toy go up, up, up. Slowly breathe out, and watch the toy go down, down, down.

★ Repeat for at least thirty seconds. With continued practice, your child may be able to practice diaphragmatic breathing independently for a few minutes.

REFLECTION AND LEARNING QUESTIONS
★ Was this kind of breathing easy or hard to do?
★ Does this breathing feel different than your normal breathing?
★ How does your body feel now that we've finished?

"LOOK FOR THE HELPERS"

The classic quote from Mister Rogers often goes viral online after a tragic event, encouraging children to look for the grownups who can help in times of crisis. Inspired by that quote, this activity helps children identify people in their network who can help them stay physically and emotionally safe.

Age Range:	**5–9**
Skills:	**Self-reflection**
Materials:	**Paper, colored pencils or markers**
Number of Children:	**1+**
Where to Play:	**Inside**

BEFORE YOU START

★ If you haven't come across this quote before, you can watch the original *Mister Rogers' Neighborhood* segment on the PBS Kids website.

HOW TO PLAY

★ Share this quote from Fred Rogers:

When I was a boy and I would see scary things in the news, my mother would say to me, "Look for the helpers. You will always find people who are helping." To this day, especially in times of "disaster," I remember my mother's words, and I am always comforted by realizing that there are still so many helpers—so many caring people in this world.

★ Draw three concentric circles on a piece of paper. The smallest circle should be just a few inches in diameter, and the largest circle should take up most of the page, leaving some blank space around the corners.
★ In the small center circle, ask your children to draw themselves.
★ In the second circle, ask them to draw pictures of the helpers in their own family. These could include parents, other adults in the home, older siblings, babysitters, or even pets.
★ In the third circle, ask them to draw helpful people outside of the home. These could include extended family, neighbors, teachers, school counselors, and friends.

(continued on next page)

* Finally, identify helpers within the community, and draw them in the corners around the edge of the page. These might include doctors, EMTs, firefighters, crossing guards, or acquaintances.

REFLECTION AND LEARNING QUESTIONS

* Who could help you if you were feeling sad or mad?
* Who could help you if you were in a dangerous situation?
* What are some ways that you can help yourself?

FEEDING THE WORRY MONSTER

Writing down worries gets bothersome thoughts out of kids' heads and on to paper, which can make them feel more manageable. This craft transforms a tissue box into a monster who can gobble up the written-down worries placed inside.

Age Range:	**5–10**
Skills:	**Emotional intelligence, self-reflection, creativity**
Materials:	**Tissue box, paper and pencil, tempera paint or construction paper, markers, scissors, glue (optional: googly eyes, glitter, pipe cleaners)**
Number of Children:	**1**
Where to Play:	**Inside**

BEFORE YOU START
★ Ask your child to imagine a monster that eats worries for dinner. It loves eating worries! Talk with them about how they imagine their worry-eating monster would look.

HOW TO PLAY
★ Using the opening of the tissue box as the monster's mouth, allow your child to design their monster however they'd like, using the materials provided.
★ Once the worry monster is complete, invite your child to write or draw their worries on pieces of paper.
★ Fold up the papers and feed them into the monster's mouth for safekeeping. Let your child decide whether or not to share their worries with you.
★ Let your child know that the worry monster is available any time to eat any worries that they might have. Encourage your child to let the worries "rest" with their monster for a little while. Later, if your child would like to take the worries out and read them or talk about them again, they can. Your child may notice that the worries have gotten smaller on their own and no longer bother them.

REFLECTION AND LEARNING QUESTIONS
★ How did it feel to feed your worries to the monster?
★ Can you think of stressful times where it might help to write down your worries? For example, before bed or before going to school?

MINDFUL COCOA

Mindfulness can be practiced in all kinds of ways. Not all kids respond well to focusing on their breathing, so this activity is a good alternative. Noticing the five senses is another form of mindfulness that is made extra fun and comforting by the addition of hot chocolate.

Age Range:	**5–11**
Skills:	**Mindfulness**
Materials:	**Hot cocoa, cups, spoons**
Number of Children:	**1+**
Where to Play:	**Inside, outside**

BEFORE YOU START
★ Tell your children that today you'd like to enjoy a treat in a special way that helps you notice your five senses.

HOW TO PLAY
★ Prepare a mug of hot cocoa for each child, making sure it isn't too hot to drink right away.
★ Explain that paying attention to what we see, hear, touch, smell, and taste helps us feel calmer and more focused, and this is called mindfulness.
★ Hand out a mug of hot cocoa and spoon to each child. Ask your children to be mindful of what the cocoa looks like. What color is it? What do they notice about their cup?
★ Next, ask each child to stir their cocoa. As they do so, ask them to describe the sounds they hear.
★ Have each child gently place their hands on the mug. Being mindful of their sense of touch, ask the children to describe what they feel. Is the cup warm or cool? Rough or smooth?
★ Ask the children to lean over their mugs and inhale. What can they smell?
★ Finally, it's time to taste the cocoa. Invite your children to slowly, mindfully sip their hot chocolate and describe the flavor with as much detail as possible.

REFLECTION AND LEARNING QUESTIONS
★ What was it like to drink hot cocoa in this way?
★ Can you think of other activities you could try doing mindfully?

MUSCLE SQUEEZES

This is a kid-friendly version of a coping skill called progressive muscle relaxation. It helps your child get rid of tension they may not even realize they are holding in their body. You'll guide your child as they tense and release muscle groups, moving through the body from head to toes.

Age Range:	**5–11**
Skills:	**Relaxation**
Materials:	**None needed**
Number of Children:	**1**
Where to Play:	**Inside**

BEFORE YOU START

★ Find a time and place to practice when your child is calm. This exercise is often used for insomnia, so it works well as part of a bedtime routine.

HOW TO PLAY

★ Read the following script to your child:

Let's practice squeezing and relaxing our muscles. First, find a comfortable spot to sit or lie down. Once you're settled, close your eyes. Place one hand on your belly and take a few big, deep breaths.

Now that you're feeling a little more relaxed, let's get started. We're going to start with our hands. I want you to imagine you're holding a couple of objects that you can squeeze. Maybe it's lemons or balls of slime. Imagine you're holding one of your objects in each hand. Give it a squeeze, as hard as you can without hurting yourself. Squeeze, squeeze, squeeze...and relax. Let's try it one more time. Squeeze...and relax. Shake out your hands and let them be floppy. Do they feel different?

Next, put your imaginary objects in the crook of each elbow. Flex your arms so you squish your object. Squeeze, squeeze, squeeze...and relax. Let your arms go floppy. One more time, squeeze...and relax. Nice work!

Now, let's work on your shoulders. Raise your shoulders and try to get them to touch your ears. Squeeze, squeeze, squeeze your shoulders... and relax. One more time, get your shoulders up to your ears, and relax, letting your shoulders be loose and floppy.

(continued on next page)

Time to focus on your stomach. Pretend that someone is about to step on your stomach and tighten your stomach muscles up so they don't squish you. Squeeze your stomach muscles tight...and relax. Let your stomach be jiggly like a bowl full of jelly. One more time, squeeze...and relax, giving yourself a jelly belly.

Let's move on to your legs. Imagine your legs are like two pieces of uncooked spaghetti: stiff and straight. Stick your legs out as straight as you can and imagine you're trying to push something away from you. Push, push, push...and now let your legs become cooked spaghetti and wiggle them around. Go back to uncooked spaghetti, stiff and straight... and now let your legs be cooked spaghetti, loose and relaxed.

Now, scrunch up your feet, like you're making them into two fists. Squeeze, squeeze, squeeze your feet...and relax, imagining all your stress flowing out of your feet and into the floor. One more time, squeeze...and then relax, and let all that stress go.

One last step. I'd like you to imagine that you're holding a lemon, and you're about to take a big bite. Scrunch up your face like you just ate something really sour. Pucker your lips, shut your eyes tight, squeeze... and relax. Okay, take one more bite, squeeze...and relax, letting your whole face release.

Before we end, let's try squeezing the entire body all together three times. Face, shoulders, arms, tummy, legs, and feet. Ready? Squeeze your whole body...and relax. Squeeze again...and relax. One last time, squeeze all your muscles...and then let yourself relax, feeling all your stress melt away.

REFLECTION AND LEARNING QUESTIONS

★ How did your body feel before and after trying this?

★ Where do you think your body tightens up when you are worried or stressed?

SENSORY BOTTLE

This art activity is popular with nearly every age group. Creating the bottle is a fun sensory experience, and the finished product can be used to practice mindfulness at home or on the go.

Age Range:	**5–11**
Skills:	**Mindfulness, creativity**
Materials:	**Empty plastic bottle, glitter glue, hot water, food coloring, hot glue gun (optional: plastic beads, small plastic figurines)**
Number of Children:	**1**
Where to Play:	**Inside**

BEFORE YOU START
★ Introduce the concept of mindfulness to your child. You can explain that mindfulness means we focus our attention on something happening in the present moment, like our breath, rather than worrying about the past or future.

HOW TO PLAY
★ Remove any labels from your plastic bottle. Add enough glitter glue to fill up the bottom 1–2 inches of your bottle.
★ Add any additional plastic items. Older children may enjoy selecting colored beads to represent different aspects of themselves or different things that relax them when they are stressed. Younger children may prefer tiny plastic toys.
★ Once your child is happy with their bottle ingredients, fill the remaining space in the jar with hot water.
★ Ask your child to select a color of food coloring and add 1–3 drops. Be careful not to make the color too dark, because this can make it hard to see the glitter inside.
★ Screw the top on the bottle and ask your child to shake it until the glue and water are fully combined. Add extra water if needed.
★ When you're satisfied with your finished product, place a thin line of hot glue around the mouth of the bottle and screw the lid closed.

(continued on next page)

* Shake the bottle up, and place it on a table. Explain to your child:

When you are anxious, your thoughts swirl around in your head like the glitter in the bottle. It can make it hard to see things clearly! Mindfulness allows your thoughts to settle down and be still. Gradually, your mind becomes clearer.

REFLECTION AND LEARNING QUESTIONS

* Can you think of a time when all your thoughts were swirling around?
* What are some other things you can focus your attention on in order to be mindful?

FIRE ALARM

We spend a lot of time talking about how to cope with worries, but can worries ever be a good thing? It's important for kids to know that anxiety, like all emotions, is helpful and protective. Understanding why our brains give us worries helps those worries feel less overwhelming.

Age Range:	**6–9**
Skills:	**Emotional intelligence, self-reflection, creativity**
Materials:	**Paper plate, red and white paint, googly eyes, pen or pencil**
Number of Children:	**1**
Where to Play:	**Inside**

BEFORE YOU START
★ Ask your child what they think about worries. Are they good or bad to have? Most kids will tell you that worries are bad, but you may get an insightful answer!

HOW TO PLAY
★ Tell your child:

You might be surprised to hear that worries can be a good thing to have. In fact, it would be pretty dangerous if you never had another worry! When our brain gives us a worry, it's acting like a fire alarm: It's getting our attention to try to keep us safe. Just like a fire alarm can be uncomfortable to listen to, anxiety and worry can feel uncomfortable in the body. But it's actually just our body doing its job to protect us by saying, "Hey, this could be a problem!"

★ If your child is interested in the brain, you can explain that a tiny part of the brain called the amygdala "sounds the alarm" in our body when it senses danger.
★ Suggest to your child that you can make a fire alarm together to help them understand more about worries.

(continued on next page)

* Paint the front of the paper plate red and add a large white dot in the center to mimic a fire alarm. For extra fun, you can add googly eyes and a worried-looking mouth to give your alarm a face. While the paint dries, tell your child:

Usually, the fire alarm part of our brain is pretty good at figuring out when we're actually in danger, and sounding the alarm when we really need it. Can you think of some times when it might be good for your brain to give you worries? If you're about to try a really difficult trick on your bike, your brain might give you worries to tell you to slow down. If you're playing outside and it's starting to get dark, your brain might give you worries to make sure that you get home safely.

After someone we love dies, the world can feel less safe than it used to. Your brain just went through such a scary experience that your fire alarm gets extra sensitive for a while. It might start seeing danger every-where. You might start worrying about things you didn't used to worry about, like other people you know going away, getting sick, or dying.

It's normal to worry about this stuff. Sometimes the worries are false alarms—your brain is worrying when it doesn't need to. Other times, the alarm is too loud—there may be a little bit of truth to the worry, but it's way bigger than it really needs to be. I wonder if you can think of any worries, big or small, that you have had since your special person died.

* On the back of the paper plate, make a list of worries with your child.
* Look at the list of worries together. Decide whether each worry is a false alarm, too loud, or a reasonable worry.

REFLECTION AND LEARNING QUESTIONS
* Did you learn anything interesting about worries today?
* Do you want to talk more about any of your worries?
* What activities might help when you notice your "fire alarm" is going off too loudly or too often?

CAN CONTROL IT, CAN'T CONTROL IT

It's common to worry about things outside of our control. After loss, when kids have a heightened sense of mortality, this can manifest as fears about other people dying. This activity helps kids acknowledge what they can't control and empowers them to change the things they can.

Age Range:	**7–10**
Skills:	**Emotional intelligence**
Materials:	**Pencil and paper**
Number of Children:	**1+**
Where to Play:	**Inside**

BEFORE YOU START
★ Tell your child that there are many different types of worries. Reassure your children that it's normal to have worries, especially after someone dies.
★ Talk with your children about how we often worry about things we can't control as a way to try to make things better. You can offer examples, such as worrying about what will be on a test or getting nervous before a big trip. See if your children can come up with examples of these kinds of worries too.

HOW TO PLAY
★ Let your child know that some things in life are out of our control, and that's disappointing. However, there is usually something else we can focus our attention on that we *can* control. This may not make a problem go away, but it can be more helpful than worrying.
★ Label a column on the left-hand side of your paper "I can't control..." In it, write a list of scenarios that are outside of our control. Include big and small issues, with both everyday and grief-specific examples. Here are some to consider:
  • The weather outside
  • Getting sick sometimes
  • Other people's feelings
  • Whether or not someone likes me
  • Having to go to school

(continued on next page)

- Whether my friends can come over
- The fact that people die

★ On the right-hand side of the paper, make a column called "But I can control…" In it, make a list of factors that are in your control that can help manage the issues on the left-hand side. Make sure this list is in random order so the issues in the "I can't control…" column aren't listed right next to their related factors in the "But I can control…" column. For example:
- Taking care of my own feelings
- Finding ways to play by myself
- Washing my hands and staying home when I don't feel well
- Taking care of my health and enjoying the time I have with loved ones
- Being kind and respectful to other people
- Being flexible if I have to play inside instead
- Choosing clubs or fun activities to join after school

★ Challenge your children to draw lines to connect the issues they can't control with the factors they can control. Provide guidance or hints as needed if they get stuck.

★ Ask your children if they can come up with other examples of what can and can't be controlled in life.

REFLECTION AND LEARNING QUESTIONS

★ Do you ever worry about things that you can't control?

★ What can you say to yourself when you notice those kinds of worries?

★ What kinds of things do you or your family do that help you to stay safe and healthy?

BOX BREATHING

Box breathing is a basic breathing technique, but it's so effective that it ends up being a favorite of many children. Tracing the square helps children stay mindful, while counting each breath helps to slow breathing down.

Age Range:	**7–11**
Skills:	**Mindfulness, emotional regulation**
Materials:	**Paper, markers or colored pencils, Zoom or another video platform (if playing online)**
Number of Children:	**1**
Where to Play:	**Inside, online**

BEFORE YOU START

★ Ask your child if they have ever tried taking a deep breath when they've been anxious. Did it work? Why or why not? Tell your child you'll try a new way of doing deep breathing today that's a little different.

HOW TO PLAY

★ Select your child's favorite color from the box of pencils or markers.

★ Help your child draw four arrows forming a large square shape. Starting with the left-hand side of the box, the arrows should point in the following directions: up, to the right, down, and to the left. You should end up with a box with an upward arrow on the left side, a right-pointing arrow across the top, a downward arrow on the right side, and a left-pointing arrow across the bottom.

★ Write (or ask your child to write) the following phrases on each side of the box:
  • Left side: "Breathe in 1-2-3-4"
  • Top: "Hold 1-2-3-4"
  • Right side: "Breathe out 1-2-3-4"
  • Bottom: "Rest 1-2-3-4"

★ Model this activity first, and then let your child try independently. Start by placing your finger in the lower-left-hand corner of the box. Trace the box shape, breathing in for a count of four as you move your finger along the upward-pointing arrow.

★ Next, hold your breath as your finger moves across the top, counting to four again.

(continued on next page)

* Exhale slowly as your finger moves down the right-hand side.
* Rest with empty lungs as your finger traces the bottom line. Your finger should end up back where you started.
* Once your child has the sequence down, encourage them to practice a few times in a row.

REFLECTION AND LEARNING QUESTIONS

* How did you feel before and after you tried this activity?
* When might it be helpful to try box breathing?

....

Your child can personalize their square by adding doodles, song lyrics, or other decorations. This activity can also be combined with the Peaceful Place Artwork exercise in this chapter by using the reverse side of the paper to create a two-in-one calming tool.

....

PEACEFUL PLACE ARTWORK

This activity helps children use their five senses to create a vivid mental picture of a place that feels soothing and relaxing to them. First, a guided visualization helps children identify what they find calming. Next, creating a drawing of their chosen place provides a helpful visual reminder for future practice.

Age Range:	**7–11**
Skills:	**Relaxation, mindfulness, emotional regulation, creativity**
Materials:	**Paper, colored pencils or markers, Zoom or another video platform (if playing online)**
Number of Children:	**1+**
Where to Play:	**Inside, online**

BEFORE YOU START

★ Have a discussion with your child or children about the connection between senses and memories. Ask if they've ever heard a song, tasted a food, or smelled a scent that reminded them of a special time in their life.

HOW TO PLAY

★ Ask your child to find a position where they can relax for a minute or two with their eyes closed. If playing in person, find a spot near your child to sit and read the following script. If playing online, ask your child to get comfortable in their seat before reading.

★ Once they have settled, read the following script, pausing between directions to allow time to visualize:

I'd like you to think of a place that makes you feel relaxed, peaceful, and happy whenever you visit it. This can be a place you go often, a special place from a vacation, or even an imaginary place from a movie or fairy tale. What's most important is that it makes you feel calm. Let me know when you've thought of your place by raising your hand.

Great! Now, let's try to make your picture of this place feel as real as possible. You get to decide what kind of place this is, and it can be however you want it to be. First, take a look around and notice what this place looks like. What colors do you see?

(continued on next page)

Next, take a moment to focus on what you can hear. What kind of sounds are in this place? Now, take a deep breath and notice what you can smell. What does the air smell like here? Wiggle your toes and notice what the ground feels like under your feet. Is there anything you can reach out and touch?

Finally, pick a food or drink you would like to have with you in your peaceful place. Imagine what it tastes like.

We're about to leave this peaceful place for now, but you can come back to visit in your imagination any time you want. Say goodbye to your place for now, and on the count of three, open your eyes. 1...2...3.

★ After your children have opened their eyes, ask them to draw what they saw on paper. Since we want this picture to be an ongoing reminder for using this relaxation skill, it's best if children complete their drawing on paper even if playing with you online.

★ If you're playing with multiple children, it can be fun to share these drawings with each other.

REFLECTION AND LEARNING QUESTIONS

★ Can you tell me about your peaceful place?

★ Why did you choose this place?

★ How did you feel before we tried this activity, and how do you feel now?

★ Can you think of a time when you could imagine your peaceful place to help you feel calm?

THE GRIEF WORRY BRAIN

This activity opens up conversations about the worries your child may experience as part of the grief process. By first imagining what worries another child might have, you give your child permission to share fears that might otherwise feel too scary to talk about.

Age Range:	**8–11**
Skills:	**Emotional intelligence, self-reflection**
Materials:	**Pen and paper, Zoom or another video platform (if playing online)**
Number of Children:	**1**
Where to Play:	**Inside, online**

BEFORE YOU START

★ If playing online, decide who will be in charge of drawing and writing. Think of some worries, big or small, that you can use as examples on your turns.

HOW TO PLAY

★ Draw a silhouette of a child's face in profile and add a large brain shape inside the head. Tell your child: "We are going to imagine all the worries that might fill up a child's brain. All kids worry sometimes. Can you think of some worries that a kid might have?"

★ Take turns naming worries a child could have and writing them down inside the brain. There's no need to push your child to share or "claim" certain worries during this activity. Allow your child to share at the pace that feels comfortable to them. You can always return to this activity on another day and explore worries again.

★ Once you've taken a few turns sharing general worries, ask your child to imagine the kind of worries a kid might have after the death of a loved one. Continue until the brain is full. Observe with your child how tough it would be to have a brain so full of worries!

★ Look at all the worries you came up with together. Ask your child if any of these worries are true for them too. Ask your child to cross out any worries that they don't experience and to circle the worries they do.

REFLECTION AND LEARNING QUESTIONS

★ How can worries cause problems for a kid?
★ Do you think it's common for kids to feel worried after a loved one dies?
★ What do you like to do when you are feeling worried to help yourself feel better?

CHAPTER 6

COPING WITH ANGER

Anger is a very common emotion for children to feel while grieving. We often get angry when we feel we aren't in control, and there are few things in life as outside of our control as death. This anger can point in many directions: Children might be angry with doctors or nurses for failing to save their special person. They might be angry with family members who they wish had been able to do more to help. They may blame themselves and direct their anger inward. Some children might express anger toward God for allowing such a bad thing to happen, or even anger toward their deceased loved one for leaving them behind.

Even though it's normal to feel angry, this can be a harder emotion for both care-givers and children to handle. Kids are often taught that being angry is aggressive or "not nice." Part of your job in this chapter's activities is to embrace your child's feelings of anger so they know it's okay to be mad. You'll find activities that help your child express and work through their anger in safe ways so those feelings don't get bottled up. You'll also find coping skills your child can use to cool down when anger becomes too overwhelming to handle.

SALT DOUGH SMASH

There's something about play dough that's satisfying when you're mad. It's squishable, smashable, and poundable, and you can mold it into anything you want it to be. Making salt dough is a fun sensory experience. Playing with it can help young children express and work through anger without the need for words.

Age Range:	**5–7**
Skills:	**Sensory grounding, creativity**
Materials:	**For dough: white flour, salt, water, measuring cup, mixing bowl (optional: food coloring); to play: kitchen utensils; for example, forks, rolling pins, spoons, spatulas**
Number of Children:	**1+**
Where to Play:	**Inside**

BEFORE YOU START
★ Salt dough can be prepared in advance and stored in the refrigerator for up to a week.

HOW TO PLAY
★ Make your dough by combining 2 cups of white flour and 1 cup of salt in a mixing bowl. Gradually add 1 cup of cold water to your dry ingredients while stirring.
★ If you're using food coloring, add a few drops of your chosen color.
★ Keep stirring until the dough begins to form, at which point you can pass it off to your helpers to knead it. If the dough seems too wet, add a bit more flour. If it's too dry, add a bit more water.
★ Gather your kitchen tools, and let your child pound, squish, squeeze, and mash the dough however they'd like.
★ You can guide your children to try different ways of handling the clay if they are feeling angry, such as punching, pounding, or throwing it against the table. It can also be fun to create bugs, monsters, or other creatures that can be squashed by a spatula, rolling pin, or fork.

REFLECTION AND LEARNING QUESTIONS
★ How does it make you feel to play with clay?
★ Everybody gets mad about stuff sometimes. Is there anything that's made you mad lately?

MAD PICTURE

A picture is worth a thousand words, particularly for young children who struggle to verbalize big feelings like anger. Drawing a picture of what makes them angry discharges angry feelings without having to say them out loud. Ripping and crumpling paper are good alternatives for showing anger in a way that doesn't hurt others.

Age Range:	**5–7**
Skills:	**Emotional regulation, creativity**
Materials:	**Paper, crayons or markers**
Number of Children:	**1**
Where to Play:	**Inside**

BEFORE YOU START
* Remind your child about the difference between real and pretend when it comes to being angry. It's *not* okay to say or do mean things to a person in real life when you are mad, but drawing an angry picture doesn't hurt anyone, so it's okay to do.

HOW TO PLAY
* The next time your child is feeling mad, encourage them to try drawing a picture of what is upsetting them and how they feel about it. Tell your child to draw or write things down on their paper rather than showing their anger by yelling, hitting, or stomping.
* Once your child is satisfied with their drawing, they can choose what to do with it. For example, they can keep it in a private place to look at later, rip it up, step on it, or crumple it up and throw it in the recycling bin. Anything that doesn't hurt other people or damage their belongings is okay to do.
* Keep an eye on your child to ensure that destroying their picture is providing a release, rather than bringing up stronger feelings. If you sense your child is having a hard time regulating their feelings, redirect to another coping skill to help them unwind.

REFLECTION AND LEARNING QUESTIONS
* How did your body feel when you were angry?
* How did you feel after you finished your mad drawing?
* Is there anything else you wish we could crumple up and throw away?

DRAGON BREATHS

Children who are reluctant to try deep breathing may be enticed by the idea of becoming a fire-breathing dragon!

Age Range:	**5–7**
Skills:	**Emotional regulation, relaxation, creativity**
Materials:	**Toilet paper tube, markers or paint, googly eyes, pom-poms, red construction or crepe paper, scissors, glue**
Number of Children:	**1**
Where to Play:	**Inside**

BEFORE YOU START

★ Talk about the difference between deep belly breathing and chest breathing. You can try the Beanbag Breathing activity in Chapter 5 to notice the difference.

HOW TO PLAY

★ Tell your child you'll be making a dragon out of the craft supplies, then breathing like one. Have the child decorate their toilet paper tube with markers or paint. The tube will become the body of the dragon.

★ Glue two googly eyes to two pom-poms. Glue these pom-pom eyes to the top of the tube body, about one-third of the way down the tube. Glue two pom-poms near the end of the toilet paper tube to create nostrils.

★ Cut the construction or crepe paper into several strips of long fringe. Roll these strips up and glue one end to the inside edges of the tube to create fire coming out of your dragon's mouth.

★ Once your glue has dried, have them hold the back end of the toilet paper tube to their mouth so the paper fringe hangs out the front. Read the following script:

Imagine that you are a dragon, and your mad feelings are burning in your belly like fire. Take a deep breath in through your nose and fill your belly up with air. Breathe in until your belly is big and round. Now, breathe that fire out through your dragon mouth. Give me a dragon roar when you do it: rahhhhhhhh! Let's try this a few more times until we've breathed all our fire out, and our bellies feel nice and cool.

REFLECTION AND LEARNING QUESTIONS

★ How did it feel to breathe like a dragon?
★ Can you notice yourself starting to cool off when you breathe?

WORKOUT WHEEL

Anger-coping strategies like punching a pillow don't work well for all kids. Overall, activities that expend pent-up energy without aggression tend to work better. In this activity, kids will identify a handful of cardio and strength exercises to deal with anger and organize them in a fun spinning-wheel form.

Age Range:	**5–9**
Skills:	**Emotional regulation, self-reflection, creativity**
Materials:	**Paper plate, metal brad, construction paper, scissors, colored pencils or markers**
Number of Children:	**1**
Where to Play:	**Inside**

BEFORE YOU START

★ Ask your child to describe what it physically feels like when they become angry. Where does your child feel anger in their body? What are the first signs that they're starting to get mad?

HOW TO PLAY

★ Tell your child:

Have you ever noticed that when you feel really mad, you get a big surge of energy? Think about what happens to the Hulk. When he's mad, he gets bigger and stronger and goes on a rampage and smashes everything. He hulks out! That kind of happens to us too.

When we are mad, our brains figure that we must need to protect ourselves or fight something, and so it sends a whole bunch of energy and strength to the body. It leaves us feeling hyped up, and we have to let that energy out somehow in order to feel better.

Sometimes people punch, kick, and stomp when they're mad. These activities burn up energy but don't help get rid of anger entirely. Your brain notices you're still doing angry actions, so it thinks you need even more anger to keep going. Can you think of some exercises you could do instead if you needed to burn up extra energy?

* Divide your paper plate into either four or six sections by drawing two perpendicular lines (for four sections) or an X plus a vertical line (for six sections). You should end up with a design that looks like slices of a pie.
* Have your child help you pick out some physical activities that could expend extra angry energy. The best activities tend to be simple to perform, don't require a lot of equipment, and can be done in a variety of settings. If your child has a favorite sport, you can incorporate that as well. Here are a few to get you started:
  * Jumping jacks
  * Push-ups
  * Take the dog for a walk
  * Run laps around the house
  * Shoot baskets
  * Burpees
  * Yoga or stretching
  * Jogging in place
* Ask your child to help you write and illustrate each of their choices in one slice of the pie.
* Cut an arrow shape out of your construction paper and affix it to the center of your wheel by poking a hole in the middle of the plate and connecting the arrow to the plate with your brad. A loose attachment is better, because it will help your arrow be able to spin more easily.
* The next time your child is feeling mad or frustrated, encourage them to give the wheel a spin and try the activity the arrow lands on. If that one doesn't sound good in the moment, spin again!

REFLECTION AND LEARNING QUESTIONS

* Do you think it's ever a good thing that we get all this angry energy sometimes?
* Have you ever tried any of these activities when you were angry?
* If you've tried some of these before, how did they work?
* What could you add or change to make your exercises easier or more helpful when you're mad?
* Where should we keep your wheel so you can find it easily when you need it?

SCREAM BOX

Sometimes, kids (and adults) just need to scream. This art redirects a child's impulse away from screaming at a person and toward something more playful. The paper inside the box helps to muffle sound so that others in the house are less likely to be disturbed.

Age Range:	5–10
Skills:	Emotional regulation, creativity
Materials:	Cereal box, paper towel tube, pencil, cellophane tape, scissors, newspaper, decorations of choice (e.g., stickers, construction paper, markers)
Number of Children:	1
Where to Play:	Inside

BEFORE YOU START
★ Remind your child that anger is a normal, healthy part of life, and it's totally understandable to feel mad after a loved one dies. We just need to find healthy ways to let it out.

HOW TO PLAY
★ Use your paper towel tube to trace a circle in the middle of the top flaps of your cereal box. Cut out this circle so you have a hole at the top of the box.
★ Crumple up your newspaper and stuff it into the cereal box.
★ Insert your paper towel tube into the hole, and seal the box shut with tape.
★ Your child can use whatever art materials you have on hand to decorate and personalize the scream box.
★ The next time your child is angry, they can try screaming into the tube, and notice how the sound gets "trapped" by the box.

REFLECTION AND LEARNING QUESTIONS
★ How do you feel after using your scream box?
★ Did your anger get bigger or smaller?
★ Can you think of any times recently when you just wished you could scream?

Some kids may find that screaming makes their anger bigger, not smaller. Check in with your child about how they are feeling.

COPING CORNER

Sometimes, the more time we spend trying to reason with a child about what's making them upset, the bigger their anger or frustration grows. Designing a special place where kids can go to soothe their anger independently helps kids feel empowered rather than punished for their feelings.

Age Range:	5–1
Skills:	Emotional regulation, sensory grounding, self-reflection
Materials:	Pillows or blankets, sensory items, art materials, books or toys
Number of Children:	1+
Where to Play:	Inside

BEFORE YOU START

★ Talk with your child or children about the purpose of a coping corner: It's a place where kids can choose to go when they're feeling overwhelmed, angry, or frustrated. It gives children a place where they can calm down and have some time alone.

HOW TO PLAY

★ Choose a location for your coping corner with your children. If multiple children will be sharing the space, a central location makes sense. For one child, a bedroom is often a natural choice. Many children enjoy an enclosed space, such as a closet, a tent, or a corner that's shielded from view by furniture.

★ Brainstorm items that would make the corner feel comfy and cozy. Blankets, pillows, stuffed animals, or a beanbag chair are all good options.

★ Choose at least one item that can be used for sensory-based soothing, such as a fidget toy, scented lotion, sensory bottle (see Chapter 5), or a no-mess alternative to slime such as Mad Mattr or Crazy Aaron's Thinking Putty.

★ Pick at least one quiet activity that can be calming and distracting, such as a picture book, coloring book, or puzzles like crosswords or Mad Libs.

★ Consider adding something that can help burn off excess energy indoors in a safe way, such as a jump rope, exercise ball, or squeezable stress ball.

★ Your child might also enjoy having materials on hand that are safe to destroy, such as Bubble Wrap to pop, egg cartons to rip, or newspaper to shred.

(continued on next page)

* A prop that encourages belly breathing can also be helpful. A pipe-cleaner flower or small toy for Beanbag Breathing (both in Chapter 5) can work well here, and a pinwheel could also promote deep, full breathing.
* Finally, ask your child if there's anything else they'd like to have on hand that would help their corner feel personal to them. Older children might appreciate having a journal to write in, while kids of all ages may enjoy decorating their space.
* Remind your children that the coping corner is not a punishment: They can choose to go to the corner whenever they feel they could use a break.

REFLECTION AND LEARNING QUESTIONS

* What are some examples of times when you might want to use your coping corner?
* Can you name some things or situations that often make you feel angry?
* What are your first warning signs that anger is starting?
* How will you know when you're calm and ready to leave?

Caregivers may worry that leaving to use a coping corner could give children an "out" from finishing arguments or accepting consequences. Pausing to use coping skills doesn't give children a pass for whatever was happening beforehand. Instead, they help a child calm down enough to think clearly and resolve the conflict in a better way.

UN-FAVORITE MEMORY

The death of a loved one often triggers an outpouring of positive sentiments, both at the funeral and in following months. This can give children the impression that it's no longer okay to express negative feelings about the deceased. By openly discussing less-than-positive memories, you can give children a safe place to express anger.

Age Range:	**5–11**
Skills:	**Emotional intelligence, self-reflection, creativity**
Materials:	**Paper; crayons, markers, or colored pencils**
Number of Children:	**1+**
Where to Play:	**Inside**

BEFORE YOU START
★ Ask your child or children if they remember any stories loved ones shared about their special person during the eulogy or in the time following the death.

HOW TO PLAY
★ Tell your children:

When a person we love dies, it is normal to want to talk about all the good things about them and the good times that we shared together. There are so many things we will miss about them. But I bet you have some not-so-favorite memories too. Maybe there was a time you got into a fight with your special person, or they did something you didn't like. It's okay to talk about those times too. It doesn't change the love we feel.

★ Ask each child to draw a picture of an "un-favorite" memory with their loved one. This can be something big or small, as long as it is meaningful to them.
★ Ask each child to either write a few sentences about their picture or dictate the story to you.
★ Ask your child to tell you the story of what happened and describe their picture to you.
★ If your children feel comfortable sharing with each other, hearing about other people's "un-favorite" memories normalizes that we can both love and be mad at people at the same time, even after death.

(continued on next page)

REFLECTION AND LEARNING QUESTIONS

* What was it like thinking about this memory?
* If you could tell your special person anything about this memory, what would you say?
* It's possible to love somebody and be mad at them too. Can you think of other opposite feelings you might have at the same time?

SPRAY AWAY ANGER

Many kids love drawing on a whiteboard and then using a spray bottle to dissolve their drawing. It's a chance to express anger without hurting anyone's feelings, and a powerful metaphor for washing away past upsets and starting fresh.

Age Range:	**6–11**
Skills:	**Creativity**
Materials:	**Whiteboard, dry-erase markers, spray bottle, water, paper towels**
Number of Children:	**1**
Where to Play:	**Inside, outside**

BEFORE YOU START

★ Remind your child that saying, doing, and thinking things when you play, pretend, or draw doesn't hurt a person or their feelings. Play is a safe place to let anger out.

HOW TO PLAY

★ You and your child will take turns drawing pictures on the whiteboard of things you feel mad about after your loved one's death. Ask your child whether they would like to start or have you go first. You can use one of the following prompts as a jumping-off point, or create your own:
  • Something unfair about my loved one dying
  • Something I wish my loved one and I had gotten to do
  • Somebody who doesn't understand my feelings
★ After you draw your picture, you can add or change anything you'd like to about it.
★ If you've drawn a picture of a person, it's okay to talk to the picture as if they were really there. Remind your child that since this is just make-believe, it's okay to say things that aren't polite.
★ When you've said everything you'd like to say, spray your spray bottle at the whiteboard and watch your drawing melt away.

REFLECTION AND LEARNING QUESTIONS

★ Was this activity easy or hard for you?
★ How did it feel to spray your picture away?
★ How are you feeling now?
★ Did you say anything to your drawing that you wish you could say in real life?

"BUT IT'S UNFAIR!"

We spend a lot of time in "normal" life telling children why things that seem unfair really aren't so bad. When it comes to a death, however, things really *are* unfair. Sometimes just saying those things out loud helps kids feel a bit better.

Age Range:	6–11
Skills:	Emotional intelligence
Materials:	Paper and pen
Number of Children:	1
Where to Play:	Inside

BEFORE YOU START
★ Validate that it's okay to feel like death is unfair. Both kids and adults struggle with anger about it, and it's common to ask, "Why me?"

HOW TO PLAY
★ Draw a line down the center of your paper to form two columns. Title the left-hand column "It's unfair that…" Encourage your child to list as many unfair situations related to the death as they can think of. (Either one of you can write them down.)
★ Once your child has run out of ideas, move on to the right-hand column. Title this column "I wish I could…" Ask your child to express what they wish they could do about each unfair situation, even if it's not possible to do it in real life.
★ Empathize with your child. You can help them identify feelings by making statements such as "I would feel so frustrated if that happened to me," or just validate their feelings by saying something like "You are right, that is really not fair."

REFLECTION AND LEARNING QUESTIONS
★ How did it feel to say these things out loud?
★ Do you have any leftover mad feelings after writing this down? If so, how can we help you let them out?

Not everybody in a child's life will understand what it's like to have a loved one die. To take this exercise a little deeper, ask your child if there's anything they wish friends, family, or teachers understood about grief.

GRIEF ICEBERG

For grieving children, anger is often just the tip of the iceberg. Even though anger is what we see, other emotions, like sadness and fear, may be lingering just below the surface, like an iceberg that is mostly under the water. This activity takes this famous metaphor from the Gottman Institute and relates it specifically to grief.

Age Range:	**7–11**
Skills:	**Emotional intelligence, self-reflection**
Materials:	**Blue and white construction paper, pen or marker, cellophane tape, Zoom or another video platform (if playing online)**
Number of Children:	**1**
Where to Play:	**Inside, online**

BEFORE YOU START
* Explain the metaphor "the tip of the iceberg" to your child. Have a conversation about how most of an iceberg exists deep below the water, where it can't be seen.

HOW TO PLAY
* Tell your child that, sometimes, anger is like an iceberg. Suggest that today you try an activity to see what anger and icebergs have in common.
* Ask your child to create an iceberg by crumpling up pieces of white construction paper and taping them to a sheet of blue construction paper. Their iceberg should take up most of the page, with a smaller tip at the top of the page and a large base toward the bottom.
* Draw a squiggly line near the top of the page to indicate the waterline and show how much of the iceberg pokes up above the water.
* Tell your child:

It's not fun to feel angry, because it doesn't feel good in our bodies. But all feelings are important and helpful, even uncomfortable ones like anger. Feelings are our body's way of sending us a message and getting us to pay attention to things.

(continued on next page)

When a person is grieving, they may feel angry a lot. The anger is like the tip of the iceberg—it's the feeling that is easy for us to notice. But underneath that anger there might be a whole lot of other feelings, hidden away deep down. Anger lets us know that we should go looking for those other deep feelings to figure out what's causing us to feel so bad.

* Ask your child to draw some symbols for anger around the top of the iceberg; for example, mad faces, dragons, or a person striking an angry pose.
* Tell your child:

The feelings below the surface of our anger might be hard or scary for us to show to other people. Sometimes, that's why they stay hidden. A person might feel jealous, worried, sad, hurt, embarrassed, disappointed, or many other feelings underneath their anger.

* Brainstorm additional feelings with your child. Write these feelings words down on scraps of paper and tape them to the bottom of the iceberg. Here are a few other feelings to consider if your child needs help brainstorming: lonely, offended, feeling things are unfair, guilty, left out, or tired.
* Ask your child to illustrate some of your brainstormed feelings around the bottom of the iceberg.
* Ask your child to imagine what situations might make grieving kids angry. Can they think of examples? What feelings might be underneath their anger, and why?
* Next, ask your child to think of a recent time when they felt angry. What happened? Think about what was visible "on top of the iceberg," such as yelling, frowning, or arguing. Ask your child to name or guess what feelings might have been happening "beneath the surface."
* If you have a recent example of your own, it can be helpful to share with your child so they understand that anger is a normal, healthy reaction to grief.

REFLECTION AND LEARNING QUESTIONS
* What did you learn during this activity?
* Are there places or times when you find yourself getting angry a lot?
* What below-the-surface feelings might you have during those times?
* What might your mad feelings be trying to tell you?

ANGER MANTRA

A little bit of encouraging self-talk can help kids stay grounded when they get angry, giving them a moment to pause and reflect instead of losing their cool. Choosing a mantra in advance takes the guesswork out of finding a helpful statement the next time a child is angry.

Age Range:	**8–11**
Skills:	**Emotional regulation, self-reflection**
Materials:	**Paper, scissors, pen, cellophane tape**
Number of Children:	**1+**
Where to Play:	**Inside**

BEFORE YOU START

★ Define what a "mantra" is for your child or children. For the purposes of this exercise, you can say that it's a phrase you repeat to yourself to help you stay calm and focused.

HOW TO PLAY

★ Begin by brainstorming a list of as many positive affirmations and helpful sayings as you can. If you're playing as a group, encourage all children to participate in creating this list. To help get your children started, here are some common sayings that work well for this exercise:
  • This, too, shall pass.
  • Let it go! Let it go!
  • When life gives you lemons, make lemonade.
  • Tomorrow is another day.
  • There's a light at the end of the tunnel.
  • Cool, calm, and collected.
  • I will survive!

★ Talk about how quotes like these make your children feel. Calm? Thoughtful? Annoyed? Which quotes did they like, and which didn't they like?

★ Have your children try saying the quotes out loud. You might want to experiment with some silly voices or dramatic gestures. How does it feel to say these things? Even when your child is being a little bit silly, do they notice a change in their mood or energy when they speak the phrase out loud?

(continued on next page)

* Notice that none of these quotes are about solving a problem or figuring out how to handle it—that's not the point of a mantra like this. Instead, they just help you calm down your anger and refocus on what's really important. How you decide to figure out the problem is up to you.
* Next, ask your child to think up phrases they could say to themselves the next time they get angry. Add the ideas your child comes up with to your list. Feel free to share any ideas of your own. Phrases like these are often helpful for kids:
  * I can handle this.
  * This isn't worth my energy.
  * Just move on.
  * Even if it's not what I want, I am okay.
  * This won't matter tomorrow.
* Ask each child to select a phrase or saying from the list that is most appealing to them. Try saying these phrases out loud. Have your children decide which phrases feel the most natural to say, and which ones don't feel quite so natural.
* Once your children have practiced many possible mantras, have each one select the one they felt most comfortable saying. This can be one from the original list or a mantra invented by the group. It's fine to choose a mantra that was originally created by another player.
* Cut a sheet of paper into small strips (think fortune cookie size) and ask each child to write their mantra on a few of them.
* These strips can be taped to notebooks, laptops, phones, pens, desks, the inside of a locker, or anywhere else a child could use a quick reminder of their mantra. If your child isn't sure where to put their mantra, help them to mentally walk through their day. What do they do after they wake up in the morning? How does your child get ready for school? What's the most stressful part of the day, and what objects are usually around during that time?

REFLECTION AND LEARNING QUESTIONS
* What did you think of this activity?
* Sometimes when we're angry, other people say things to us like "Get over it" or "It's no big deal." How do those comments make you feel?
* How are mantras like this different than those comments?

CHAPTER 7

COPING WITH SADNESS

Sadness is the most common emotion experienced during grief, which is why we often use the word to describe feelings of despair. Some children's sadness is very visible: You may notice a lot of crying, clinging, and low mood in the days or weeks following a death. For others, sadness isn't so apparent: Children may push their feelings down and not share them with others.

Caregivers should keep an eye out for the many ways sadness can express itself. Body aches and pains, trouble at bedtime, and a lack of interest in activities can all be signs that a child is struggling with sad feelings. Just like all responses to grief, sadness is normal, understandable, and a helpful emotion to feel and express.

In this chapter, you'll find a mix of activities to help your child process and deal with sadness and guilt. When your child is ready and able to do so, creative arts activities will help them express their feelings of sadness and share them with you. When your child needs a break, activities that emphasize coping skills can help dial down the intensity of their feelings. Over time, your child can work through their sadness and find healthy ways to cope.

REMOTE CONTROL

It can be empowering for young children to discover they have some control over their strong emotions. This art project uses a remote control as a metaphor to help kids understand how coping skills can help them manage sadness and other difficult emotions.

Age Range:	**5–8**
Skills:	**Emotional regulation, creativity**
Materials:	**Cardboard, buttons or pom-poms, glue, fine-tip marker or pen**
Number of Children:	**1**
Where to Play:	**Inside**

BEFORE YOU START
★ Chat with your child about how remote controls are used. Ask them to list all the things they can do with a remote control, like turn up the volume on the TV or change to a different channel.

HOW TO PLAY
★ Tell your child:

Today, let's create a remote control for sad feelings. Sadness is an okay feeling to have, but sometimes, you might want some help changing the channel to another feeling. Other times, you might just want to turn the volume down on your sadness so that it's easier to handle.

★ Cut your cardboard into a rectangular shape with rounded edges, aiming for a size that's larger than a real remote control. A rectangle of around 4 inches by 6 inches should work well.
★ Glue four to six pom-poms or buttons onto your "remote" to resemble device buttons.
★ Brainstorm activities with your child that they might be able to use to "change the channel" or "turn down the volume" on their sadness, such as:
  • Go outside
  • Pet my cat or dog
  • Ask for a hug
  • Read my favorite book
  • Curl up with a blanket

- Dance to music
- Watch funny videos on YouTube
- Talk to a caring adult
- Draw a picture
- Play a game

★ Assign one activity to each button on your remote. Write each activity under each button for children who can read. If your child isn't reading yet, ask them to draw a picture to go along with your captions.

REFLECTION AND LEARNING QUESTIONS

★ When might you want to lower the volume on sadness?

★ When might you want to change the channel on sadness?

★ Sometimes, it feels best to let yourself feel sad and cry. When might you do that?

SPECIAL ACTIVITY CALENDAR

It is hard to work up the motivation to do good things for ourselves when we're feeling down, even if that's exactly what we need to do to feel better. Inspired by a therapy technique called behavior activation, this activity helps your child prioritize feel-good activities.

Age Range:	5–11
Skills:	Emotional intelligence, creativity
Materials:	Paper and pen or calendar template, stickers or markers
Number of Children:	1
Where to Play:	Inside

BEFORE YOU START

★ If using a premade calendar template, select one online and print before starting.

HOW TO PLAY

★ Read or paraphrase this script to your child:

When we are feeling sad, our brain plays a trick on us. It tells us that nothing we used to like is fun anymore, so we shouldn't do anything but sit around. What's tricky about this is that getting out and doing fun stuff is sometimes exactly what we need to do to feel better!

The more we sit around and do nothing, the sadder we are probably going to feel. Even if it doesn't sound very fun, we will probably surprise ourselves and find out that once we start doing it, we feel much better.

★ If you're creating your own calendar, draw or trace a grid with four rows and seven columns.

★ Brainstorm three activities to try this week. These do not have to be expensive or time-consuming. The most helpful activities are ones that are social, creative, or provide a sense of accomplishment, such as:

  • Cook a simple recipe together
  • Try a new board game
  • Movie night with a friend
  • Visit a zoo, library, or playground

- FaceTime with a faraway friend or relative
- Take a bubble bath
- Go out for ice cream

★ Select times to do these three activities and label them on the calendar with stickers or drawings. Think about your own schedule and what times you can realistically be available to support your child, if need be.

REFLECTION AND LEARNING QUESTIONS

★ Was it easy or hard to do your activities this week?

★ How did you feel before and after you tried them?

★ Which activity was your favorite?

MINDFUL NATURE SCAVENGER HUNT

Research suggests that time spent outdoors offers a range of mental health benefits, including reduced symptoms of depression, improved ability to reflect on problems, and an increased sense of connectedness. This activity encourages children to spend meaningful, screen-free time in nature, which can, in turn, help them deal with sad feelings.

Age Range:	**5–11**
Skills:	**Mindfulness, sensory grounding, self-reflection**
Materials:	**Paper and pencil**
Number of Children:	**1+**
Where to Play:	**Outside**

BEFORE YOU START
★ Remind your children that mindfulness means paying attention to what's happening in the here and now.

HOW TO PLAY
★ Identify a natural space you can take your children. If you are able to travel, it can be fun to visit a new or remote location. Otherwise, a local park or even a backyard can work just fine.
★ Tell your children that you'd like them to practice mindfulness while you explore nature together.
★ Create a list of scavenger hunt items, then review the items together. You can brainstorm together, or just make a list yourself and share it with the child. Here are some examples:
  • Something red, yellow, or orange
  • Something with an interesting shape
  • Something that smells nice
  • Something pointy, sharp, or rough
  • Something that makes a fun sound
  • Something beautiful

* Give each child the scavenger hunt list. Decide whether each child should search for their items separately, or if your children would prefer to work as a team.
* Challenge your children to find all the items on the list without talking (if playing with more than one player). If they're unable to locate a specific item, they should bring back the closest thing they can find.
* Once finished, ask children to share their discoveries with the group.
* If you'd like to continue playing, brainstorm a list of new scavenger hunt challenges with your children for a second round of the hunt.

REFLECTION AND LEARNING QUESTIONS

* What was it like to look for these items without talking?
* How does it feel to be out in nature?
* Did you see anything cool or surprising while you were on your hunt?
* Did you notice anything you might have missed if you weren't being mindful?

T-SHIRT COMFORT PILLOW

If your child had a lovie as a baby, you know the soothing power of a comfort object. Also called transitional objects, they remind a child of their parents' love when a parent can't be nearby. A pillow made from a loved one's shirt can provide similar comfort.

Age Range:	**5–11**
Skills:	**Emotional regulation, creativity, relaxation**
Materials:	**A loved one's old T-shirt, fabric shears, safety pins, cotton batting**
Number of Children:	**1**
Where to Play:	**Inside**

BEFORE YOU START

★ Select a T-shirt for this activity that you don't mind cutting into. A shirt that is familiar to your child but not an irreplaceable keepsake is a good choice.

HOW TO PLAY

★ Lay your T-shirt flat on a table or work surface. Safety pin the front and back sides of the shirt together at each shoulder and the two bottom corners to hold them in place.

★ Use your shears to cut a large rectangle or square shape out of the center of the shirt, trimming away the sleeves, collar, and hem. (If your shirt has a logo or graphic on the front, take care to leave 2–3 inches of space around it so that it is visible in the finished product.) You should be left with two identical shapes from the front and back of your shirt that will form the outside of your pillow.

★ Notch the four corners of your front and back panels by cutting a 2-by-2–inch square out of each one. You can ensure all your cutouts are identical by folding the panels into quarters before cutting.

★ Cut a fringe along all four sides of your shirt fabric, making sure to include both layers of fabric when you make your cuts. The tassels should be 2 inches long. This is the same depth as your cutouts, so you can use them as a guide.

★ The thinner your fringe, the more time your pillow will take to complete. Consider using 1-inch thickness for younger children, and 3/4- or 1/2-inch thickness for older kids.

* Now it's time to put your pillow together. Tie each tassel from your upper layer of fabric to the lower layer of fabric to form a knot. Help younger children with this task as needed.
* Continue knotting your layers together until you have almost completed all four sides, leaving a gap of a few inches to add the stuffing.
* Use this gap to stuff your pillow with cotton batting.
* Finish knotting your final few tassels to complete your pillow.

REFLECTION AND LEARNING QUESTIONS

* How did it feel to turn your loved one's shirt into something new?
* Do you remember your special person wearing this shirt?
* Where should we keep your pillow so you can have it close by?
* When might you want to hold or hug your pillow?

COMFORT MAGNET

Children of all ages should be encouraged to cry and let their sad feelings out when they need to. Creating a magnet to put on the fridge gives kids a nonverbal way to indicate they're feeling down, and they could use a shoulder to cry on.

Age Range:	5–11
Skills:	Emotional intelligence, self-reflection, creativity
Materials:	Jar lid, paper, colored pencils or markers, glue, refrigerator magnet
Number of Children:	1
Where to Play:	Inside

BEFORE YOU START
★ Tell your child: "It's always okay to cry. Sometimes, crying is our body's way of telling us we need comfort from somebody else to help us feel better. Let's make a magnet you can use to let me know if you ever need me to be with you while you're feeling sad."

HOW TO PLAY
★ Use your jar lid to trace a circle onto your paper.
★ Ask your child to decorate the space inside the circle with some sort of symbol the two of you can share, such as an emoji, that will let you know they could use your company.
★ Cut out the image and glue it to the inside of the jar lid.
★ Glue your magnet to the back of the lid. The floppy magnets used as promotions by businesses work well for this, and you can trim the magnet down to size if need be.
★ Ask your child to hold on to the magnet. They can be in charge of putting it on the refrigerator when they would like support.

REFLECTION AND LEARNING QUESTIONS
★ Have you ever noticed that sometimes crying can be a relief?
★ Whom or what do you like to have around you when you're sad?
★ Has there ever been a time when it felt like it wasn't okay to be sad or to cry?

TURNAROUND LEGOS

Children are often surprised to learn that our thoughts tell us how to feel about the world—but our thoughts aren't always totally accurate. Learning to notice and examine these thoughts is a first step toward combating the hopelessness, worry, and changes in outlook that sometimes accompany a loss. This activity uses Lego bricks to show how we can transform unhelpful thoughts by looking at them from another perspective.

Age Range:	**6–9**
Skills:	**Creativity, self-reflection**
Materials:	**Assorted Lego bricks and a large, flat Lego baseplate**
Number of Children:	**1**
Where to Play:	**Inside**

BEFORE YOU START

★ Read *Tiger-Tiger, Is It True?* by Byron Katie with your child to introduce the concept of "turnaround thoughts," the more accurate, helpful statements we can say to ourselves in order to transform unhelpful or inaccurate thought patterns.

HOW TO PLAY

★ Review the main message of *Tiger-Tiger, Is It True?* and help your children connect it to their grieving process. You can say something like:

We just learned that the thoughts we think help us decide how to feel about things, and sometimes our thoughts aren't completely true. Everybody feels like Tiger-Tiger sometimes and has thoughts that make them feel sad or lonely.

When somebody we love dies, we might feel sad, lonely, or even hopeless a lot of the time. It might even feel like nothing will ever be good again. We might feel bad about ourselves or believe that things just aren't going to work out for us. It makes sense that we'd think that way because something really terrible just happened. Have you ever had any thoughts like this?

★ Ask your child to identify a time when they've had an unhelpful thought that's led them to feel sad or hopeless.

(continued on next page)

* Sometimes, children have a hard time separating thoughts from feelings. If your child responds by saying something like "I was sad," you can rephrase by asking them what their brain was saying to them when they felt that way.
* Once your child has picked a thought, ask them to represent it by building a scene or sculpture out of Legos on one half of the large Lego baseplate. What did they imagine was going to happen? What were they thinking about themselves or other people? How did the thought make them feel?
* Once your child has finished, tell them:

Just like Tiger-Tiger, we can practice noticing these thoughts when they happen so we can decide if they're really true. We can ask ourselves questions to see if things are really as bad as they seem. We can turn our thoughts around to find something a little more true and helpful.

* Ask your child to turn their sculpture around and build a new scene on the other side of the Lego baseplate. This scene represents their turnaround thought. It can show a version of the situation that is more realistic or accurate.
* Once your child has finished, ask them to share both sides of their Lego creation with you.

REFLECTION AND LEARNING QUESTIONS
* How can you tell if a thought is true or not?
* When Tiger-Tiger thought "nobody cares and nobody likes me," he felt rotten. Have you ever felt like that?
* What is the difference between a thought and a feeling?
* What is a turnaround thought you can tell yourself if you notice a thought like this happening again in the future?

It's okay to acknowledge that there may be some truth behind a child's unhelpful thought: Overly positive thoughts aren't very realistic, either! The most helpful turnarounds show that things aren't usually as bad as they seem, and your child is capable of handling hard situations.

SADNESS MONSTER

Difficult emotions can sometimes feel like a personal flaw or a permanent part of who we are. In this activity, children imagine sadness as a monster or creature as a way of externalizing their feelings—seeing the sadness as something outside of themselves.

Age Range:	**6–11**
Skills:	**Emotional intelligence, creativity**
Materials:	**Paper; crayons, colored pencils, or markers**
Number of Children:	**1+**
Where to Play:	**Inside**

BEFORE YOU START

★ Read a storybook or browse through art with your child to make the idea of a "sadness monster" less abstract. Younger children might enjoy reading *The Color Monster* by Anna Llenas. Older kids may appreciate the illustrations in Toby Allen's *Real Monsters*, available online.

HOW TO PLAY

★ Ask your child or children to imagine what their own feelings of sadness would look like as a monster. Guide the activity and encourage exploration by asking questions such as:
   • What color would your monster be? Would it be large or small?
   • Does this monster have any special powers? How does it affect people?
   • Does this monster say anything when it strikes?
   • What does this monster like to do?
   • Does this monster have a name?
★ After brainstorming, ask your children to draw their imagined monsters on paper.
★ If you're playing in a group, invite all players to share their monsters when they've finished.

REFLECTION AND LEARNING QUESTIONS

★ What's the most interesting part of your monster?
★ What did you notice about other people's monsters?
★ Do you think these monsters can ever be helpful to us?
★ How can you help yourself when your sadness monster shows up?
★ Can you think of other feelings that you could draw as a monster or creature?

WOULDA-COULDA-SHOULDA DRAWING

It's normal for children to feel guilt and regret as part of the grief process. They may remember an argument with their loved one or a time they misbehaved when they wish they hadn't. Expressing these feelings through art and poetry can alleviate shame and help children feel less alone.

Age Range:	**7–10**
Skills:	**Creativity, self-reflection**
Materials:	**Paper; crayons, colored pencils, or markers**
Number of Children:	**1**
Where to Play:	**Inside**

BEFORE YOU START
★ Read the poem "Woulda-Coulda-Shoulda" by Shel Silverstein with your child and discuss its meaning.
★ Remind your child that many people feel guilty sometimes when they are grieving, even if they know they loved their special person and their special person loved them.

HOW TO PLAY
★ After you've talked about the poem, tell your child:

It's normal for kids and grownups to be left with lots of Wouldas, Couldas, and Shouldas after someone we love dies. We might think about all the nice things we would have told our person if we'd had more time. We might think about things we could have done differently, but maybe we were too mad or upset at the time. We might feel bad because we think we should have done something and wish we could have a second chance to make it right. Can you think of anything like that?

★ If possible, share some of your own regrets or wishes with your child related to your loved one's death. This helps to reassure children that their own feelings are normal, making it easier for them to share too.

* Ask your child to write or draw any Woulda-Coulda-Shouldas that they can think of on their paper.
* Talk with your child about their picture. It can be hard for caregivers to hear that their child has been carrying around guilt or regret. You might be tempted to try to fix the feeling right away by telling your child they have nothing to feel bad about. Instead, help your child put names to their feelings without trying to change them. If you're not sure what to say, statements like these can help validate a child's feelings:
  * "I can see why you might feel that way."
  * "It must be hard to think about that."
  * "It sounds like you might feel sad and guilty that you said that."
* Sometimes, children may express a belief that something they said or did caused their loved one to die. If your child expresses something along these lines or another similarly exaggerated thought, you can remind them that our thoughts and feelings can't ever hurt a person's body or cause them to die.
* Once you've finished talking through feelings of guilt and regret, flip the paper over. Ask your child if they can remember other times when they showed love or respect to their special person or had a very happy day together. You might also ask if there are ways that they can show love and respect to others in the future. Draw or write these memories and ideas on the reverse side of the page.
* Invite your child to talk with you about their guilty feelings any time they feel the need.

REFLECTION AND LEARNING QUESTIONS
* What did you think about this poem?
* The last line of the poem says that all the Woulda-Coulda-Shouldas ran away from one little Did. Why do you think that is?
* How do you feel now that we have finished our picture? Can we do anything else together to take care of your feelings?

JOY COLLAGE

In the middle of grief, it can be hard to remember that there are still good things in the world. By making a collage of meaningful pictures, children can take note of the things—big and small—that they can still appreciate and look forward to enjoying.

Age Range:	**7–11**
Skills:	**Gratitude, creativity, self-reflection**
Materials:	**Old magazines, scissors, construction paper or poster board, glue or glue sticks**
Number of Children:	**1+**
Where to Play:	**Inside**

BEFORE YOU START

* Validate for your child or children that it's a normal and okay part of grief to feel like things aren't much fun anymore, or that there isn't much to look forward to.

HOW TO PLAY

* Suggest to your child that today you can make a collage of things that are good or happy in the world. Explain that these can be big things, like Disney World, or small things, like chocolate chip cookies.
* Invite your children to flip through the magazines and cut out any words or pictures that seem joyful or meaningful to them. Pictures of pets, food, nature, and anything cute and cuddly are always good options.
* Have your child arrange their cutouts on construction paper or poster board however they wish, then glue them down.
* If you are making collages as a group, share your completed projects with each other.

REFLECTION AND LEARNING QUESTIONS

* What is your favorite picture in your collage?
* Are any of these pictures things you hadn't thought about in a while?
* Can we use any of these pictures as inspiration to find something joyful to do this week?
* Where should we put your collage so you can look at it when you're feeling down?

PICK-ME-UP PLAYLIST

Research supports the idea that music has a positive effect on our mood and stress levels. Tweens who are skeptical of using other coping skills are often passionate about their music, and happy to share it.

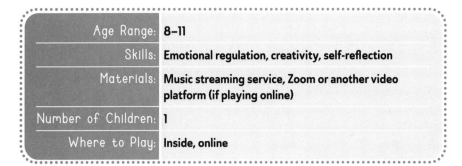

Age Range:	**8–11**
Skills:	**Emotional regulation, creativity, self-reflection**
Materials:	**Music streaming service, Zoom or another video platform (if playing online)**
Number of Children:	**1**
Where to Play:	**Inside, online**

BEFORE YOU START
★ Watch some of your child's favorite music videos or listen to their favorite songs with them. Ask your child how the music they listen to tends to make them feel.

HOW TO PLAY
★ Using whatever format your child prefers, compile a list of six to eight songs they can use to help shift out of a bad mood when they find themselves feeling down.
★ In general, up-tempo songs work best for this, though sad songs might actually make some children feel better. Search for music that feels energizing, motivating, or empowering.
★ Ask your child to share clips of each song as you add it to the list so that you can get a better sense of their taste and what's important to them.
★ If you get stuck, check out The Mighty's "Music for When You Need a Boost" playlist on Spotify. Younger kids may also enjoy Parry Gripp's songs on YouTube.
★ Once you have your list, your child can arrange the music however they like until they get a flow that feels right to them.
★ Give the playlist a cool name, and download it to your child's phone or save it on their computer so it's ready for use.

REFLECTION AND LEARNING QUESTIONS
★ How did it feel listening to this kind of music?
★ Which of these songs is your favorite, and why?
★ Can you imagine other ways that you could use music to cope with strong feelings?

YOUTUBE HELP KIT

While it's important to be able to express and work through feelings of sadness, sometimes we need to be able to get through the day or finish a task without being overwhelmed. It's okay to use distractions, like YouTube, in a strategic way to give ourselves an occasional break from tough feelings.

Age Range:	9–11
Skills:	Emotional regulation, relaxation
Materials:	YouTube, Zoom or another video platform (if playing online)
Number of Children:	1
Where to Play:	Inside, online

BEFORE YOU START
★ As with the Pick-Me-Up Playlist activity, it's helpful to prepare for this activity by getting an idea of what kind of content your child watches online. Ask your child to share some of their favorite videos with you.

HOW TO PLAY
★ Go on a hunt with your child to uncover the funniest, cutest, and most relaxing videos you can find online (that are still age-appropriate).
★ Keep going until you've compiled at least five videos, aiming for a mix of funny, cute, and relaxing content.
★ Ask your child to title their feel-good video list and save it to their YouTube profile (or somewhere else that's easily accessible).

REFLECTION AND LEARNING QUESTIONS
★ Sometimes it helps to take a short break from sad feelings. Can you think of times when it might be helpful to distract yourself for a few minutes?
★ What kinds of videos were most helpful: the cute videos, funny videos, or relaxing videos?
★ Can you think of other ways you can distract yourself when you need a break?

CHAPTER 8

HEALING THROUGH STORYTELLING

In this chapter, you'll find ways to help your child talk about their loved one's death from their point of view. Storytelling is a chance for children to put the pieces of their experience together in a way that makes sense to them. It allows children to speak directly to their loved one and express sentiments—good and bad—that they might not have had the chance to say out loud during their loved one's lifetime. It's also an opportunity for you, as a caregiver, to show your child that you can handle speaking directly about your loved one and their death, even if your child has painful feelings to share.

The goal of these activities is not for your child to relive the most difficult, painful moments of their grief story in detail. That's something that can help as a part of therapy, but only when someone can make sure a child doesn't get overwhelmed by their memories. Instead, children will use letter writing, storytelling, art, and poetry to express whatever they choose, whether it's "deep" or more surface-level. No matter what your child chooses to share, your listening, attentive presence is what matters most.

MY SPECIAL PERSON PICTURE BOOK

Stories help us make sense of the world. Your young child may have been soothed by reading picture books about grief in the early days after their loved one's death. Now it's their turn to share about grief and their special person through their own eyes.

Age Range:	**5–7**
Skills:	**Creativity, self-reflection**
Materials:	**Construction paper, white paper, stapler, pen and markers**
Number of Children:	**1**
Where to Play:	**Inside**

BEFORE YOU START

★ Consider rereading a favorite storybook about grief with your child.

HOW TO PLAY

★ Fold two white pieces of paper and one piece of construction paper in half widthwise to create a booklet with a construction paper cover and eight interior white pages. (If your child would like to write a longer story, add an additional sheet or two of white paper.)

★ Place your folded white pieces inside your folded construction paper. Place three staples alongside the folded edge to create a binding.

★ Show your child the blank pages of the book, and tell them that today, it's their turn to be an author. They are an expert about the life of their loved one, and today you'll be writing a story all about them. Tell your child that they can fill the pages with whatever writing or drawing they choose.

★ Although your child is taking the lead on what to write, you can help them find a structure for their story. Choose any or all of the following topics to include in your book, or add some of your own:

- All about My Special Person
- What I Liked to Do with My Special Person
- My Favorite Memory with My Special Person
- What Happened When My Special Person Died
- The Funeral

- How I Felt about the Death
- How I Remember My Special Person

★ Decide in what order these topics should be written. It usually makes sense to begin with more general information about your child's loved one, then move on to details of their death and your child's response. You can end with how your child memorializes their loved one or another topic that helps bring the story into the present day.

★ Once you've chosen an order, write each topic across the top of one page of the booklet to serve as a "chapter" title.

★ If your child needs help writing, ask them to dictate the text for each page of your book. Write down their responses.

★ Ask your child to illustrate each page. Allow some extra time for them to do this, as they may really like to immerse themselves in the visuals of their special person's memory.

★ Give your story a title and ask your child to draw art for the front and back covers of the book. If your child would like, they can also add an "About the Author" section on a spare interior page or on the back cover and include a self-portrait.

★ Read the story out loud with your child. You can revisit it whenever your child would like to think about their special person. Repeating the story helps your child to process the information and make sense of their loss.

REFLECTION AND LEARNING QUESTIONS

★ How did it feel to write this book?
★ Was it easy or difficult to tell this story?
★ What would you like other people to know about your special person?

Need a book on grief to read before writing your own? Read a Grief Story. Toy Funeral. Tear Soup. Life-Cycle Drawing. and Invisible String Heart Garland are all activities that include story recommendations to provide a jumping-off point for your own story.

I'M SORRY, I FORGIVE YOU

It's not always so easy to express negative thoughts and feelings about a loved one after their death. Rather than leaving these sentiments unsaid, young children can express apologies or let go of grievances through art to achieve a sense of closure.

Age Range:	5–9
Skills:	Creativity, emotional intelligence, self-reflection
Materials:	Paper, crayons or markers, Zoom or another video platform (if playing online)
Number of Children:	1
Where to Play:	Inside, online

BEFORE YOU START

★ Talk about the meanings of apologies and forgiveness with your child, if needed.

HOW TO PLAY

★ Let your child know that it's normal to wish we had said or done things differently with our special person while they were alive. It's also normal to wish they had said or done things differently too.

★ If you have any child-appropriate examples of apologies you wish you could have made or received from your child's loved one, it can be helpful to share them.

★ On one side of the paper, ask your child to draw a picture of something they wish they could apologize to their loved one about. It can be something big and important or something small and unimportant.

★ If your child is old enough to write, ask them to write their apology in words somewhere on the paper. If not, they can dictate their apology to you.

★ Ask your child to draw a picture on the reverse side of the paper of something they would like to forgive their loved one for having said or done.

★ If your child is old enough, they can write a statement beginning with "I forgive you for..." on this side of the sheet. If not, they can dictate their statement to you.

★ Ask your child to tell you about their pictures and read their statements.

REFLECTION AND LEARNING QUESTIONS

★ What was it like to draw these pictures?

★ Is there anything else you would like to say sorry to our loved one about?

★ Is there anything else you'd like to forgive?

ONE PERFECT DAY

This activity is a little different than the others in this chapter. Rather than sharing memories and past experiences, you'll invite children to imagine a future with their loved one. Children can express unresolved hopes and wishes.

Age Range:	**5–11**
Skills:	**Creativity, imagination**
Materials:	**Art supplies, pen and paper or word processor, Zoom or another video platform (if playing online)**
Number of Children:	**1**
Where to Play:	**Inside, online**

BEFORE YOU START

★ Ensure that younger children understand the permanence of death before beginning this exercise. Otherwise, it may be confusing to imagine a day when a loved one could return from the afterlife.

HOW TO PLAY

★ Tell your child:

We know that in real life death is permanent. Today, though, I'd like you to imagine that you got to spend one perfect day with your special person, and then tell me a story about what you would do. Because this is a magical and imaginary situation, you can do anything you want.

★ Give younger children the choice to either act out their story or illustrate it and dictate the words to you. Older children can write and illustrate on their own. Alternatively, for online play, older kids can use a word processor and use clip art to illustrate their story.

★ Ask younger children to speak their story out loud as they act it out or explain their story to you. Older children can read the story aloud.

REFLECTION AND LEARNING QUESTIONS

★ What do you miss most about being with your special person?

★ We can't make this story happen, but maybe we can find something that we can try in real life. Are there any activities we could do to help you feel closer to your special person?

BEFORE AND AFTER FAMILY PORTRAITS

Grief stories don't need to be complex. Portraits are a simple, powerful way for young children to express the changes they've seen and felt in their family. Older children sometimes appreciate taking a break from words to express themselves through art too.

Age Range:	**5–11**
Skills:	**Creativity**
Materials:	**Paper and drawing materials, Zoom or another video platform (if playing online)**
Number of Children:	**1**
Where to Play:	**Inside, online**

BEFORE YOU START

★ Select your art materials. Young children may enjoy crayons, markers, or tempera paint. Older children often enjoy watercolors or colored pencils.

HOW TO PLAY

★ Tell your child: "I'd like you to make two pictures of our family: one of us before our loved one died, and one of us after."

★ Support and observe your child as they complete their two portraits in their medium of choice.

★ If your child asks you for feedback, try not to make assumptions about what you're seeing. Instead, make "I notice..." statements to encourage your child to share more about their artwork and feelings. For example, "I notice that you used a whole lot of red over here" or "I notice that Daddy is really tall, and everyone else is very small."

REFLECTION AND LEARNING QUESTIONS

★ What is different about our family since our loved one died?

★ What has stayed the same?

★ Whom did you feel closest to in the "before" picture? Whom do you feel closest to now?

★ If you put a speech bubble above each person's head, what do you imagine they would say?

★ How do you imagine this portrait would look if you drew it a year from now?

ACROSTIC NAME POEM

This activity uses the structure of an acrostic poem to help children verbalize import-ant feelings, traits, and memories they associate with their loved one. It may be par-ticularly helpful for kids who struggle with more open-ended prompts.

Age Range:	**7–11**
Skills:	**Creativity, self-reflection**
Materials:	**Paper; colored pens, pencils, or markers; Zoom or another video platform (if playing online)**
Number of Children:	**1**
Where to Play:	**Inside, online**

BEFORE YOU START

★ Describe what an acrostic poem is to your child. You can explain that these poems are special because the first letter of each line spells out a word or phrase. Each line of the poem has something to do with that word.

HOW TO PLAY

★ Ask your child to write the name of their special person vertically down the left-hand side of the page. They can choose to use a full first, middle, and last name; simply a first name; or the name they used for their loved one.

★ Help your child come up with a sentence describing their loved one that starts with each of the letters of their name. If your child needs inspiration, consider the following prompts:
  • A personality trait or physical characteristic
  • A funny thing about them
  • Something they were very good at (or not very good at)
  • Their favorite food, movie, hobby, or song

★ Your child can illustrate their poem if they'd like, either with decorations or by adding a portrait of their loved one.

★ When the poem is completed, ask your child to read it aloud to you.

REFLECTION AND LEARNING QUESTIONS

★ How did it feel to write this poem?
★ Which line is your favorite?
★ Did you remember anything new about your special person while writing this?

LETTER TO MY LOVED ONE

Writing a letter directly to a deceased loved one gives children an opportunity to put unsaid feelings into words they didn't get a chance to share in life, which can help provide a sense of completion or closure. The process of writing and reviewing also allows a child to reflect on their own grief process.

Age Range:	**7–11**
Skills:	**Creativity, emotional intelligence**
Materials:	**Pen and paper or word processor**
Number of Children:	**1**
Where to Play:	**Inside**

BEFORE YOU START

★ Help your child figure out how they're most comfortable writing. Some children enjoy writing by hand, while others prefer to type. A Word document, Google Docs, or a dedicated email account are good options for this.

HOW TO PLAY

★ Find a time when your child would like to express their feelings to their loved one, and set them up to write in their preferred format.

★ Your child can begin their letter by addressing it to their loved one.

★ Your child may have their own ideas about what they'd like to write. If they're feeling stuck, offer the following sentence stems to complete:
- I still remember...
- The best thing you taught me was...
- I loved it when you...
- I didn't like when you...
- I wish I could change...
- It's not fair that...
- It still bothers me that...
- Thank you for...

★ Ask your child to share their letter with you, ideally by reading it aloud. If your child feels strongly about keeping it private, that's okay, but in general children get more benefit by sharing their thoughts with others.

* Ask your child how they'd like to "send" their message. They can save their letter or find a symbolic way to transmit it, such as burning it or folding it into a paper boat and letting it float away.

REFLECTION AND LEARNING QUESTIONS

* What was it like writing this letter?
* Did it bring up any feelings for you?
* Do you need any support from me?

UNSENT TEXTS

Using the familiar structure of a text message, this activity gives older kids a chance to express sentiments that were left unsaid when their loved one died. By imagining what their loved one might say in response, children can gain a sense of closure on this unfinished business.

Age Range:	**8–11**
Skills:	**Self-reflection, emotional intelligence**
Materials:	**Pen and paper (optional: printed template)**
Number of Children:	**1**
Where to Play:	**Inside**

BEFORE YOU START

★ If you're able, search on Google or Pinterest for "text message template" in advance and select an option to print for use in this activity.

HOW TO PLAY

★ If you're using a template, be sure you have a copy printed out. If not, turn your paper vertically (portrait orientation) and ask your child to draw a large phone with a blank screen, taking up most of the paper.

★ Tell your child that after a loved one dies, there are often things we wish we could have said to them, but we never had the chance to. These might be apologies, things they said or did that we didn't like, or things we appreciated about them but never shared with them directly.

★ If you'd like, you can share any of your own age-appropriate sentiments that you wish you'd shared more directly with your deceased loved one. Any sort of personal sharing from you will make it easier for kids to share their own thoughts and feelings, so you could share an example if you want. If you need examples, here are a few to consider:

• Apologizing for not seeing them as often as you could have

• Thanking your family member for a tradition they passed down, such as a special recipe

• Giving a compliment about something you never had a chance to share in life

* Tell your child that today, you'll imagine you could put those unsaid thoughts down in a text to send to your loved one. Because this is a text instead of a conversation or a letter, you can have the best of both worlds; you can really think about what to say, but it can still be short and sweet.
* Ask your child what they would want to say if they could send a message like this. They can write their message down on the template or on their drawing.
* After they press "send," ask your child how they imagine their loved one would respond. What kind of text does your child think they would send back?
* As your child imagines their response, you can draw the familiar "dot dot dot" that you see when you're expecting an incoming text.
* Ask your child to write their imagined response on the template or on their drawing.
* If your child would like, they can continue this conversation back and forth, sharing any other thoughts that arise, until they feel they've reached the end.
* Ask your child to find a way to end this text conversation. How should they say goodbye for now?
* Ask your child to read or share their text conversation with you.

REFLECTION AND LEARNING QUESTIONS
* What was it like to do this activity?
* How are you feeling now that we've finished?
* Do you ever imagine having conversations with our loved one, or imagining what they might say to you?
* What was it like to imagine getting a response to your text?
* Are there any other messages you wish you could send, either to our loved one who died or to other people in your life?

MY SPECIAL PERSON COMIC STRIP

This is a variation on the My Special Person Picture Book activity that might be better suited for older children who like comic strips.

Age Range:	**8–11**
Skills:	**Narrative creation**
Materials:	**Online comic maker like Pixton or StoryBoard That, Zoom or another video platform (if playing online)**
Number of Children:	**1**
Where to Play:	**Inside, online**

BEFORE YOU START
★ Online comic makers have a learning curve, so practice in advance.

HOW TO PLAY
★ If you are playing in person, sit with your child as they create their comic strip panels. If you're playing online, decide who should be in charge of controlling the mouse and creating the comic strip.
★ Ask your child to create a comic telling the story of their special person that has a beginning, middle, and end. You can use the prompts from the My Special Person Picture Book activity as a jumping-off point. If your child is motivated to continue past those topics, here are others to consider:
  • What my special person was like as a child
  • My favorite memory with my special person
  • Things my special person and I have in common
  • Something I miss about my special person
★ Allow your child the time they need to let their comic reach a natural conclusion.
★ Ask your child to share their finished comic with you.

REFLECTION AND LEARNING QUESTIONS
★ Which panel is your favorite?
★ How did you choose characters to represent everyone in the story?

It's okay if your child's memories of what happened aren't completely accurate. You don't need to correct errors like mixed-up dates unless they're causing your child distress.

HAIKU EPITAPH

For children who struggle with open-ended prompts, the structure of a haiku can provide a safe container for creative expression. The short and simple nature of this poetry encourages the writer to think about the most essential part of their message.

Age Range:	**8–11**
Skills:	**Creativity**
Materials:	**Pencil and paper or word processor, Zoom or another video platform (if playing online)**
Number of Children:	**1**
Where to Play:	**Inside, online**

BEFORE YOU START
★ Gather examples of haiku poetry and epitaphs to share with your child. A haiku is a special kind of Japanese poem with only three lines. The first line has five syllables, the second line has seven syllables, and the third line has five syllables.

HOW TO PLAY
★ Introduce the activity by talking with your child about epitaphs. You can say something like "An epitaph is a short sentence or phrase that honors a person who has died. You might see an epitaph engraved on a tombstone."
★ Discuss how epitaphs usually summarize something important about the life of the special person who has died. They can be serious, sweet, or silly, just like the people they honor.
★ Suggest to your child that today you create an epitaph for your loved one, using the form of a haiku to guide you.
★ If your child gets stuck, you can help them think of synonyms that fit the haiku format. In the end, your child's message is more important than the number of syllables, so don't feel like you have to keep too close an eye on the form.
★ Invite your child to read their finished haiku aloud to you.

REFLECTION AND LEARNING QUESTIONS
★ What style did you choose for your haiku? Is it serious, silly, or something else?
★ Why did you pick this style?
★ How did you decide what was most important to include in your haiku?
★ If you could engrave this epitaph somewhere, where would you put it?

GRIEF STORY PLAYLIST

This online-friendly activity helps tweens tell the story of their grief process nonverbally. Musically minded kids may enjoy creating a soundtrack for their experiences, which can lead to eye-opening conversations.

Age Range:	10+
Skills:	Creativity
Materials:	Music streaming service, Zoom or another video platform (if playing online)
Number of Children:	1+
Where to Play:	Inside, online

BEFORE YOU START
★ You can warm up to this activity by asking your child or children to share some of their favorite music videos or artists they're currently listening to.

HOW TO PLAY
★ Review the common phases of grief with your child: shock, denial, bargaining, guilt, anger, depression, and hope. Remind your child that not everybody goes through every stage or does so in order.
★ Ask your child to select one to two songs to represent each stage of grief that feels personally relevant to them.
★ Once they have gathered their songs, they can arrange them in order to tell the story of their grief process, adding any other songs that have emotional significance or that remind them of specific moments.
★ Invite your child to share their playlist with you. Your child can explain why they've chosen each song and what moment in time the song corresponds with.
★ Take note of the genres of music your child has chosen to tell their story. Do the music styles change over time? Do the lyrics seem especially poignant or powerful? Do any of the songs remind you of your loved one? Observations like these can lead to deeper conversations with your child about their story.

REFLECTION AND LEARNING QUESTIONS
★ What made you choose this song? The melody, the lyrics, or something else?
★ What would you title this playlist?
★ If you could pick a song to represent how you feel today, what would it be?

CHAPTER 9

KEEPING MEMORIES STRONG

When a person dies, the relationship we had with them doesn't go away—it just changes. Even though your child can't see their loved one anymore, they are still filled with thoughts, feelings, and memories about them that need someplace to go. This chapter's activities help your child find a way to maintain a bond with their special person even though they're no longer physically present.

Here, you'll find activities that help your child understand that love continues after death. You'll find many ways that you and your child can keep the memory of your loved one alive, both individually and as a family. Art activities give children tangible reminders to hold on to, and rituals help kids and families comfort each other as they mark special occasions, such as holidays, without their loved one present.

When you encourage your child to memorialize your loved one, you're letting them know that it's okay to still think about them. You're giving your child ways to revisit their connection with their loved one when they need to, even months or years from now. And, just as importantly, you're reminding your child that it's normal to remember people we've lost, and that you remember them too.

INVISIBLE STRING HEART GARLAND

The Invisible String by Patrice Karst is a classic book for bereaved children. It teaches that love between children and their special people endures regardless of distance, angry feelings, and even death. The activity that follows helps children remember this invisible connection with loved ones.

Age Range:	**5–8**
Skills:	**Creativity, emotional intelligence**
Materials:	**Red or pink construction paper, hole punch, fishing line, two key chain rings, photos or art supplies**
Number of Children:	**1**
Where to Play:	**Inside**

BEFORE YOU START
★ Read the book *The Invisible String* with your child, taking time to reflect and answer any questions that arise.

HOW TO PLAY
★ Help your child make a list of special people or pets they love who would be connected by their invisible string. Aim for five to ten special people.
★ Cut out one pink or red construction paper heart for each name on your list.
★ Using your hole punch, make two holes on either side of the top of each heart.
★ Ask your child to draw a picture of each person or pet onto one of the hearts, or glue photos of your special people to the hearts.
★ Cut about 2 feet of fishing line and tie a key chain loop to one end of the line.
★ Help your child string their hearts along the fishing line.
★ Finish the garland by tying the second key chain loop to the other end of the fishing line.

REFLECTION AND LEARNING QUESTIONS
★ Do you think a person's love goes away when they get angry at someone?
★ Sometimes, things might make us feel a tug on the invisible string we have with our special person who died. What makes you feel a tug on the string?
★ Where should we put your garland so you can remember your string?

MEMORY TABLE

Inspired by Pixar's movie *Coco*, this activity adapts one of the movie's key traditions to make it accessible for kids of all ages and cultures. Children will explore the mixed feelings that can come up during grief and reflect on why it's important to remember and talk about the dead.

Age Range:	**5–11**
Skills:	**Emotional intelligence**
Materials:	**Surface such as a shelf or table inside your child's home, candles, flowers, mementos from your child's special person**
Number of Children:	**1+**
Where to Play:	**Inside**

BEFORE YOU START

★ Watch the movie *Coco* alongside your children so you are familiar with the story and can answer any questions that arise. The movie contains some fantasy elements that may be confusing for younger children who are still working on understanding death. If you think your child may have trouble separating reality from fantasy, you may want to begin just by showing a video of "Remember Me," a song from the end of the film.

HOW TO PLAY

★ After watching the film or film clip, talk with your children about Día de Muertos if it is not a holiday you celebrate. You can say something along the lines of:

Día de Muertos means "Day of the Dead" in Spanish. It's a holiday in Mexico where people remember and celebrate their family members who have died. It's a special and happy time, because they believe the spirits of their ancestors are close by.

During Día de Muertos, families make a special altar called an ofrenda *as a gift to their loved ones. They fill it with pictures, flowers, candles, and many things that their special people loved while they were alive.*

We don't celebrate Día de Muertos, so we don't need an ofrenda. *But we can make a special memory table to celebrate and remember our special person on any day we like.*

(continued on next page)

* Choose a place in your children's home to create a memory table, such as an empty shelf on a bookcase or an end table.
* Decide with your children what items should be on your memory table. Think about objects your loved one enjoyed or would find beautiful, such as:
  * Small statues, trinkets, or treasures belonging to your loved one
  * Flowers or sweet-smelling items
  * Colorful objects in your loved one's favorite colors
  * Food and drink your loved one enjoyed (or representations of them)
  * Items related to your loved one's hobbies
  * Small collectibles such as toys or action figures
  * Framed photos
  * Religious symbols (angel statues, crosses, etc.)
  * Battery-operated candles
* Help your children gather their chosen items and arrange them until they are happy with their creation.
* Take a moment to enjoy your memory table together by lighting the candles and playing "Remember Me" or another song of your choice.

REFLECTION AND LEARNING QUESTIONS

* In Mexico, Día de Muertos is a happy holiday with lots of celebrating. Does that surprise you? Why or why not?
* Miguel's family tried hard not to remember their great-grandfather for a long time. Why can remembering be difficult to do?
* Miguel says we don't have to forgive our loved ones, we just need to not forget them. Can you be angry and miss someone at the same time?
* What was it like to hear Miguel's family talk about the dead? Is it different than how we talk about the dead in our family?
* How do you hope to be remembered someday?

Coco is a children's movie. but it has important messages for grownups too. Miguel is affected by the adults in his life. who avoid talking about his great-grandfather. Even though Miguel isn't able talk about his great-grandfather with his family. we see that he still thinks about him. He doesn't have information. so he comes up with his own ideas about who his ancestor must be.

DESIGN A MEMORIAL SERVICE

Research shows that asking children what they would have changed or added to a loved one's funeral service helps them to better remember the event as they grow up. Imagining and illustrating their own memorial service gives children an opportunity to creatively express their own values.

Age Range:	5–11
Skills:	Self-reflection
Materials:	Paper; crayons, colored pencils, or markers
Number of Children:	1
Where to Play:	Inside

BEFORE YOU START

★ Consider your timing before introducing this activity. It helps to wait until some time has elapsed (at least three to six months) since the memorial service before reflecting on the experience.

HOW TO PLAY

★ Tell your child that you'd like to hear their point of view on their loved one's memorial service.
★ Review some of the basics of the experience: Where did it take place? Who attended? What rituals happened during the service in order to honor your loved one?
★ Tell your child:

I want you to imagine that you got to be in charge of designing the memorial service. Let's pretend all the choices had been up to you. You could add or change anything you wanted about it. In this imaginary world, there are no limits or rules about what you could spend, create, or do. If it were all up to you, how would you have wanted the service to be?

★ If your child would like to explore more before drawing, help them think about any or all of the following:
  • Where would the funeral or memorial take place?
  • What kind of music would you play?

(continued on next page)

- How would you want to remember your special person?
- What colors or objects would you use to decorate?

★ Ask your child to put their ideas on paper by drawing an illustration of what the memorial service or funeral would look like.

★ Ask your child to share their finished picture with you.

REFLECTION AND LEARNING QUESTIONS

★ What parts of your special person's memorial service did you like and want to keep the same?

★ What parts of the funeral did you not like and want to change?

★ What do you remember the most about the day?

FAMILY REMEMBRANCE RITUAL

Rituals help grievers of all ages process feelings of grief. They mark important milestones, provide a safe space for feelings, and help survivors feel closer to their lost loved one. Children benefit from the sense of control over their world that comes from creating a ritual of their own.

Age Range:	**5–11**
Skills:	**Emotional intelligence, cooperation, creativity**
Materials:	**Optional: App for playing music or other media, photos of loved one, musical instruments**
Number of Children:	**1+**
Where to Play:	**Inside, outside**

BEFORE YOU START

★ Define what a ritual is for your child. For example: "A ritual is a special routine that helps us remember and share feelings about a person who has died. Rituals can help us stay close to our special person and each other."

HOW TO PLAY

★ As a group or family, devise a ritual that you can use to remember your loved one at special times. You can use your creativity to combine elements that were meaningful to your loved one into something you can all enjoy together. This could be a regular occurrence, like a moment of pause before you sit down for family dinner, or something more sporadic, like a semiannual visit to the grave site or a place your loved one enjoyed. The ritual should have a beginning, middle, and end that stays the same every time you meet.

★ Begin by deciding when the ritual should take place. Ask your children if they would like to plan on holding this ritual every week, meeting once a month, or perhaps only using the ritual to remember their special person on special occasions, like holidays or anniversaries.

★ Next, decide where the ritual should take place. Common locations for rituals include the family home, the grave site, or near a memorial tree.

★ Decide on a beginning for your ritual. Some ideas to consider are:
  • Saying a prayer together
  • Reading a favorite poem

(continued on next page)

- Lighting a candle
- Ringing a bell or chime

★ Choose a middle for your ritual. You can choose a simple, short activity or something longer depending on how often you plan to practice it, such as:
  - Watching a loved one's favorite TV show or movie
  - Singing or playing a song together as a family
  - Listening to your loved one's favorite music
  - Eating your loved one's favorite food
  - Taking turns talking to your loved one

★ Decide how your ritual should come to an end. This may be similar to your beginning, such as sharing a final prayer, snuffing out a candle, or ringing a bell for a second time.

★ Every family member should give input when creating the ritual and decide on the elements together. Each person should also have a specific role or job to do within the ritual itself.

★ Choose a time to try out your ritual for the first time. Feel free to make changes and allow the ritual to evolve once you see how it feels.

REFLECTION AND LEARNING QUESTIONS

★ How do you feel about trying out our ritual as a family?
★ When should we practice our ritual for the first time?
★ Do you have any other ideas to add to make this ritual special?

MEMORY BOX

Memory boxes are helpful for grieving people of all ages. They can be especially comforting for children, who use tangible objects as a way to "hold on" to connections with loved ones. The box can remind children of details that might otherwise be lost to time as they grow older.

Age Range:	**5–11**
Skills:	**Self-reflection**
Materials:	**Small box, mementos**
Number of Children:	**1**
Where to Play:	**Inside**

BEFORE YOU START

★ Go shopping for a jewelry or storage box with your child or decorate an upcycled box to make it feel special.

HOW TO PLAY

★ Gather special items to place in the box. These do not have to be valuable, but they should trigger a strong, positive memory for your child of their special person. Consider adding some or all of the following:
  • Something your loved one liked to wear
  • Something with your loved one's handwriting on it
  • Something representing a favorite hobby, trip, or activity
  • A photo of your child and their loved one
  • Something with a scent that reminds you of your loved one
★ Ask your child to write (or have them dictate to you) a message to include for each item in the box explaining its significance. This can help spark your child's memory as they grow, reminding them of why these objects are so special.
★ Remind your child that they can open up this box whenever they would like to feel close to their loved one. When they have finished, they can close the box and put it away for another time.

REFLECTION AND LEARNING QUESTIONS

★ Which item is your favorite?
★ Did you remember anything new about your special person as we put this box together?

FIVE SENSES MEMORIES

This online-friendly group activity works well for impromptu sharing with groups of mixed-age children. Thinking about the five senses may help kids make new associations or bring up new memories about their loved one.

Age Range:	**5–11**
Skills:	**Communication**
Materials:	**Zoom or another video platform (if playing online)**
Number of Children:	**1+**
Where to Play:	**Inside, outside, online**

BEFORE YOU START

★ Find a time to play when conversation has already turned to memories of your loved one. Because no materials are needed, this activity works well on Zoom, during car rides, and other times when most play activities are not possible.

★ If needed, review the five senses for younger players.

HOW TO PLAY

★ Tell your children that the five senses are very good at helping us to remember things. Suggest that you try as a group to come up with sights, smells, tastes, feelings, and sounds that remind you of your loved one.

★ Take turns going around the group, asking children to name a sense memory that falls into one of the five categories. Some examples might be:

- The taste of a loved one's favorite food
- The smell of food cooking or a loved one's perfume
- The feeling of a familiar piece of clothing
- The sound of a loved one's humming or singing
- The sight of a loved one's car

★ Try to name at least one memory for each of the five senses.

★ Continue for as many rounds as you'd like.

REFLECTION AND LEARNING QUESTIONS

★ Did anybody name a memory you hadn't thought about in a while?

★ Which sense memory was your favorite?

★ How can we use our senses to help us remember our special person? For example, should we wear their favorite color or listen to their favorite song today?

HOLIDAY REMEMBRANCE ORNAMENT

Holidays like Christmas can be especially difficult for young grievers, who have to navigate this emotional, family-oriented time of year without their loved one nearby. Creating a Christmas ornament can help your child keep their special person's memory close during the holiday season.

Age Range:	**5–11**
Skills:	**Creativity**
Materials:	**Polymer clay or salt dough, cookie cutters, rolling pin, toothpicks, baking sheet, ribbon or yarn (optional: food coloring, clay tools, printed photos, Mod Podge)**
Number of Children:	**1+**
Where to Play:	**Inside**

BEFORE YOU START

★ You may want to explore your child's feelings about the upcoming holiday season before beginning this activity. How will this year be different without your loved one?

HOW TO PLAY

★ If using polymer clay, warm it up first by rolling and kneading it in your hands. This will make it pliable and ready to use. Polymer clay will allow your children to create more detailed, longer-lasting ornaments and is a good option for older kids. If using salt dough, follow the recipe from Salt Dough Smash in Chapter 6, which only requires white flour and salt to make and may be easier for younger children to handle. Salt dough will result in simpler, more fragile ornaments.

★ Have each child choose a cookie cutter to use as the base shape for their ornament.

★ Roll the clay flat with your rolling pin, aiming for the clay to be about 1/4 inch thick. Cut out a shape for each child.

(continued on next page)

* If your child needs inspiration, here are some ideas to commemorate their special person:
  * Their loved one's name or first initial
  * Their loved one's favorite hobby
  * A symbol that represents a special tradition shared with their loved one
  * A heart or candle to represent love and memory
  * A photograph of their special person: This will need to be added after the ornament has baked
* If desired, use additional clay colors to add decoration to the ornaments. You can purchase multiple polymer clay colors, or dye parts of your batch of salt dough with food coloring. Your children can also use toothpicks or clay tools to press designs or write letters in their clay.
* Use a toothpick to create a small hole at the top center of each ornament.
* As children are working on their ornaments, preheat your oven. Set it to 250 degrees for salt dough, or follow the instructions on your packaging for polymer clay.
* Transfer your finished ornaments to a baking sheet and bake in the oven until hardened, using the instructions on your clay package as a guide.
* Once ornaments have hardened and cooled, thread yarn or ribbon through the hole to create a loop for hanging.
* If you're adding a photo to your ornament, use Mod Podge to glue the photo in place, and then cover with additional Mod Podge to seal.

REFLECTION AND LEARNING QUESTIONS
* What do you remember about celebrating the holidays with our special person?
* What will be different about the holidays this year?
* What will be the same?
* Can you name one thing you're looking forward to this holiday?
* Can you name one thing you'll miss?

MEMORIAL TREE

Planting a tree or perennial flower is an activity the whole family can participate in together. Trees symbolize hope and healing, and watching a tree grow over time can help children reflect on how their relationship with their loved one may also expand and change.

Age Range:	**5–11**
Skills:	**Emotional intelligence**
Materials:	**Tree, perennial flower, or other long-lived plant**
Number of Children:	**1+**
Where to Play:	**Outside**

BEFORE YOU START

★ Think about options for trees and planting locations that are realistic for your situation, climate, and budget. Who will be responsible for taking care of your tree once it is planted? Some parks, cemeteries, and other public green spaces offer this service for a fee, or you can plant your tree at home and care for it yourself. If it's cost-prohibitive to plant a large tree, small perennial plants such as your loved one's favorite flower or shrub can also work well for this activity. Avoid plants that only live for a season.

HOW TO PLAY

★ Have a conversation with your children about the idea of planting a memorial tree or plant. Ask your children what kind of planting would be meaningful to them. Some reasons people might choose to plant a tree include:
  • Doing something kind for the planet and others in honor of a loved one
  • Adding something beautiful to the home that represents your special person
  • Creating a special place where you or others can go to remember your person
★ Once you've discussed what's important to your children, think about whether you'd prefer to place your tree or plant at home or in a public space, such as a park.
★ Select a tree or plant. You want to find something that is long-lasting, and that is hardy and easy to care for in your area. Consider choosing a plant that was a favorite of your loved one.

(continued on next page)

* Think about other additions that might make your tree special, such as a plaque, a place to sit, or decorations created by your children.
* Use the planting of your tree as an opportunity to share memories about your loved one, read a poem, or play their favorite song. If you've completed the Family Remembrance Ritual earlier in this chapter, it could be useful here.
* Make regular visits to your new tree or plant with your children.

REFLECTION AND LEARNING QUESTIONS

* How do you think our tree will grow and change over time?
* What do you think it will be like to watch our tree grow?
* Will other living beings get to enjoy our tree?
* What can we do together to remember our loved one when we visit the tree?

Be careful about planting trees in locations such as schools where there isn't a designated person to keep up the memorial. It can be distressing for children to return to a memorial site to discover their tree has died or the memorial is in disrepair. When in doubt, stick with something small and manageable that you feel confident you can enjoy for many seasons to come.

FAMILY STORY COOKBOOK

No matter what your culture or nationality is, you can probably think of a few foods that trigger memories of family and home. This activity works online or in person to help children remember their loved one and hopefully gather a few new stories about them along the way.

Age Range:	**5–11**
Skills:	**Organization, communication, creativity**
Materials:	**Paper and pen or computer, Zoom or another video platform (if playing online)**
Number of Children:	**3+**
Where to Play:	**Inside, online**

BEFORE YOU START

★ This activity works best with support from multiple adults in your children's extended family or friend network. It is a good idea to reach out to them in advance to make sure they're available to talk with your children.

HOW TO PLAY

★ Tell your children that you'll be sending each of them on a mission to find recipes for a special cookbook dedicated to their loved one.

★ Assign each child one or more of the following categories to investigate:

- A food your special person loved as a child
- Your special person's favorite food
- A food used to celebrate holidays with your loved one
- Your special person's favorite birthday treat
- A food that brings up a funny memory or story about your loved one
- Your child's favorite food their special person cooked
- A food that reminds another family member of your loved one

★ Ask your children to speak to a relative or friend to get more information about the assigned food and any memories or stories connected to it.

★ Help your children write down the information they've learned and create a recipe for the dish. This can be an authentic family recipe, if one exists, or a re-creation of a special food using recipes found on the Internet.

(continued on next page)

* Compile the recipes and stories into a cookbook to share with your children, as well as the family and friends who helped you create it. If you have the recipes on a computer, you can save your completed book as a pdf document to share with family members, or have it printed into a physical book using a company like Shutterfly or Canva.

REFLECTION AND LEARNING QUESTIONS

* What is something new you learned during your interview?
* Which food is your favorite?
* How can we use these foods to celebrate and remember our special person?

WINDOW IN MY HEART

This activity is inspired by a line in a poem by Rumi that reads: "Your body is away from me / but there is a window open / from my heart to yours." Children can use this metaphor to explore how emotional and spiritual connections remain even when physical closeness is no longer possible.

Age Range:	5–11
Skills:	Self-reflection, creativity
Materials:	Clear contact paper, magazines, different colored tissue paper, scissors, photo or art supplies
Number of Children:	1
Where to Play:	Inside

BEFORE YOU START

★ Read the short poem "The Window" by Rumi with your child. Talk about what the poem might mean. What does it mean to have a window open in your heart? Suggest that today you think about some of the ways you can keep the window in your heart open for your loved one.

HOW TO PLAY

★ Think out loud with your child about the things they can do when they would like to feel a connection with their special person. This could include visiting certain places, eating special foods, or participating in activities that help your child feel closer to their loved one.

★ Cut out pictures from magazines to represent these things. If your child can't find the image they're looking for, they can also search online and print out the images they'd like to use.

★ Print a small photo of your special person or ask your child to draw a small portrait of them.

★ Cut two matching heart shapes out of the contact paper. You can make these hearts any size you would like, but 6–9 inches is a good ballpark size.

★ Peel the backing off one of your contact paper hearts, and place the heart sticky-side up.

(continued on next page)

* Place the photo or drawing of your special person in the center of the heart. Surround the photo with your child's cutouts. You may want to help younger children with this step, because it is difficult to rearrange cutouts once they've been stuck to the paper.
* Cut small (roughly 1-inch) strips of various colors of tissue paper. Layer these across your contact paper heart to fill in the blank spaces between your images. The finished product should resemble stained glass.
* Peel the backing off your second heart. Help your child carefully place this heart sticky-side down on top of your images to seal and finish their project.
* Hang the completed heart in a window, either in your child's bedroom or somewhere that your child can look at it regularly.

REFLECTION AND LEARNING QUESTIONS
* The man who wrote this poem, Rumi, was a Persian poet who lived over eight hundred years ago. Do you think people in different times and places have felt the same grief feelings?
* If you could send a message from your heart to your special person's heart, what would you say?
* Who can you talk to if you want someone to help you feel close to your loved one?

Poetry, music, and other forms of art are generally helpful for reconnecting bereaved children with their emotions. However, art created by grieving people—like this poem—can be especially powerful. It reminds children they aren't alone and offers hope: These artists have survived their difficult experiences and transformed them into something meaningful.

POSTCARD UPDATE

Your child's relationship with their loved one could shape the person they become, and in this way their relationship continues on even after a loved one dies. As children grow, they may wish they could share their new experiences with their special person. This activity helps children maintain an ongoing dialogue with a loved one's memory.

Age Range:	7–11
Skills:	Creativity, self-reflection
Materials:	Postcard or blank card stock, pen and colored pencils
Number of Children:	1
Where to Play:	Inside

BEFORE YOU START
★ This activity works well as a follow-up to Letter to My Loved One in Chapter 8. Consider trying that activity, which focuses on expressing unresolved thoughts and feelings, before beginning this one, which highlights new growth and milestones in a child's life.

HOW TO PLAY
★ Let your child know that it's normal to find themselves feeling more emotional or thinking about their loved one often around big life events. Validate that we all wish we could share those special times with loved ones who have died, and that sometimes writing to our loved ones can help to get our feelings out.
★ If using a premade postcard, select one with your child. The postcard can represent what your child will be writing about, such as a recent vacation or celebration, or it can just be a card your child imagines their loved one would have liked.
★ If creating a card, trim your card stock into a 4-by-6–inch rectangle. Ask your child to draw a picture on the front side of the card.
★ Start by having your child address the postcard to their loved one, using whatever name your child called them by.

(continued on next page)

* If needed, help your child write down their message. Older children may be able to do this step independently and may prefer some private time to write.
* Your child can write postcards about anything that is on their mind. A recent family trip, a holiday, or a personal achievement might all be good reasons to write a card. If your child needs help getting started, consider the following prompts:
  - I wish I could tell you...
  - I wish you could have seen...
  - I'm proud to share that...
  - I was thinking of you recently when...
  - I wonder what you'd say about...
* Invite your child to read their postcard to you if they would like.
* Ask your child to choose a sign-off for their postcard. How would they like to say goodbye?
* Ask your child how they would like to "send" their postcard. They can do this in a symbolic way, such as burning or tearing up their postcard, or they can save their postcards in a special place to look at later.

REFLECTION AND LEARNING QUESTIONS
* If your special person could answer you, what do you think they'd say?
* What was it like to write this message?
* How are you feeling after finishing your postcard?
* Would you like to do anything special to honor your loved one, since they can't physically be with us today?

Bereaved children may feel singled out on occasions that involve family participation, like school events, graduations, and parties. This is especially true if a child has lost a parent and has to spend time around peers who get to celebrate with both caregivers. It's okay to "wonder aloud" about whether your child feels this way around big events and to validate their feelings.

MEMORY NECKLACE

Making a necklace gives a child a wearable, visible connection to their loved one. Tweens often enjoy creating jewelry, and it offers a more grown-up way to hold on to memories than other crafts in this book. Plus, there's something really soothing about repetitive, fine-motor tasks like stringing beads.

Age Range:	**8–11**
Skills:	**Creativity**
Materials:	**Embroidery floss or elastic cord, assortment of beads and charms**
Number of Children:	**1+**
Where to Play:	**Inside**

BEFORE YOU START
★ Decide whether to complete this activity in or outside of the home at a bead store. Going to a bead store is a fun option, but getting some craft store supplies for at-home play is fine too.

HOW TO PLAY
★ Ask your child to choose beads that represent aspects of their relationship with their loved one. Some children may enjoy making their own associations and won't need much structure to guide them as they create their piece.
★ If your child needs extra guidance, use any or all of the following prompts to help. Ask your child to find beads or charms that can represent the following about their loved one:
- Favorite food
- Favorite sports team
- Favorite holiday
- Favorite pet or animal
- A personality trait
- Favorite band or type of music
- Your child's favorite activity to do with their loved one
- Something their loved one was good at
- Their birthplace or where they lived
- Something your child learned from their loved one

(continued on next page)

- A shared interest
- A special memory

★ Add any other beads needed to round out the design. If you have created necklaces as a group activity, take a moment to share your finished pieces with each other.

REFLECTION AND LEARNING QUESTIONS

★ Can you think of times when it might be helpful to wear your necklace as a reminder of your special person?

★ Which bead or charm is your favorite one, and why?

★ Did anybody else choose a bead that you liked too? What about it did you like?

CHAPTER 10

MAKING MEANING

This chapter contains activities to help your child discover and create meaning after loss. In Chapter 3, your child developed a factual understanding of death. In this chapter, we'll move beyond "just the facts" to consider what this death, and death in general, means for the rest of your child's life.

Making meaning is different than saying "everything happens for a reason" or justifying why a loved one died. It's a way of reflecting on everything that has happened and deciding what you can take away from it. Children can name what matters most to them about the way their loved one lived. They can think about who they are now, and how that's different from the person they were before the death. They can even explore how the death has changed the way they think about life, and how they would like to spend their life.

These are deep questions, even for adults, and there are no easy or correct answers. We also can't force another person to create meaning—it happens on its own schedule. Instead, you'll find exercises here that gently explore life after loss from a variety of perspectives, to help your child draw their own conclusions.

SIDEWALK ART

Sidewalk artists create beautiful works of art knowing that they won't last forever. Children have a chance to reflect on how experiences can have beauty and value that lasts even after they're gone.

Age Range:	5–9
Skills:	Creativity, emotional intelligence, self-reflection
Materials:	Sidewalk chalk
Number of Children:	1+
Where to Play:	Outside

BEFORE YOU START
★ Ask your child or children if they've ever seen sidewalk art. What was it like to see beautiful art out on the street? You can show them pictures of sidewalk art on your phone or computer if you need examples.

HOW TO PLAY
★ Ask your children what they imagine it is like to be a chalk artist who makes art that gets washed away. Why might they do it? What might be fun about it?
★ Suggest that today you try an experiment and make some chalk art of your own.
★ Find a place outside to create your chalk art. The ideal spot is public enough that others can appreciate your drawing, and exposed enough to the elements that rain will eventually wash it away.
★ Encourage your children to make their chalk art detailed and special, even though it won't last.
★ Take a moment to appreciate and praise your children's artwork.
★ See how many other things you can name that are beautiful and impermanent, such as sandcastles, rainbows, and ice sculptures.
★ Continue appreciating your art as it fades or washes away.

REFLECTION AND LEARNING QUESTIONS
★ Who will get to see your art? Did you enjoy making it even though it won't last forever?
★ How did it feel to see your art fading away?
★ What do you think this activity can teach us about what happens when a loved one dies?

WHAT'S DIFFERENT, WHAT'S THE SAME?

If you only have a few minutes or limited supplies, this activity works for kids of all ages, online or in person. Children get a chance to reflect on the recent changes in their lives, while also reinforcing their sense of security by remembering life's constants.

Age Range:	**5–11**
Skills:	**Self-reflection**
Materials:	**Paper and pencil, Zoom or another video platform (if playing online)**
Number of Children:	**3+**
Where to Play:	**Inside, online**

BEFORE YOU START
★ Decide how to play. Younger children can draw or dictate to you, and older children may prefer to write on their own. If you're playing online, many children enjoy using the chat function to create lists like these, especially if they can use emojis.

HOW TO PLAY
★ Begin by asking one of your children to name something that has changed since the death of their loved one. Take a minute to talk about how this death has affected everyone, and give other children a chance to add to the suggestion if they'd like.
★ Ask the same child to identify something that has stayed the same. It helps if this second statement is somehow related to the first, such as "Auntie picks us up from school now instead of Grandma, but we still have our afternoon snack and TV time every day when we get home." However, the statements don't have to relate.
★ Go around in a circle until each child has had a few opportunities to share.

REFLECTION AND LEARNING QUESTIONS
★ What is something you miss about our life before our special person died?
★ What has stayed the same that you are happy about?
★ How are you the same as and different from before the death?
★ Can you think of anything we used to do before the death that we could get back to doing now?

GRIEF EXPERT

Children love taking on the role of "expert" and sharing knowledge with others. After living through the difficulty of grief, they have learned a lot. This lighthearted role-play helps children reflect on their growth and newfound understanding.

Age Range:	**7–10**
Skills:	**Self-reflection, emotional intelligence**
Materials:	**Toy microphone (a makeshift one is fine), Zoom or another video platform (if playing online)**
Number of Children:	**1+**
Where to Play:	**Inside, online**

BEFORE YOU START

★ Think about how you'd like to frame a mock interview with your child or children. Any setting that appeals to your family and lets your child take on a position of authority works well.

HOW TO PLAY

★ For this activity, you'll be taking on the role of the interviewer. Using your toy microphone to direct conversation, interview your participating "experts" about their knowledge of grief. Players could be talking with a radio host, on a favorite talk show, or perhaps at a school assembly speaking directly to other children.

★ Inquire about the advice they would give to other children just starting out on their grief journey. Some questions to consider:
  • What is grief?
  • What kind of feelings might a grieving person experience?
  • What, in your opinion, is the hardest thing about grief?
  • What has helped you to manage your feelings?
  • What is important for a grieving child to know?
  • Do children ever have any misunderstandings about grief?
  • If a child is having a hard time, whom should they talk to?

REFLECTION AND LEARNING QUESTIONS

★ How was this interview for you? Was it easy or hard?
★ What do you think it would be like for a grieving kid to hear information like this?
★ Did anybody else give an answer that surprised you or made you think?

PHOTO FAMILY TREE

Whether our loved ones passed on physical traits from the genes they shared or personality traits from the care they gave us, we carry parts of them into the future. A family tree lets kids reflect on the concept of ancestors and how we remain connected to those who came before us.

Age Range:	**7–11**
Skills:	**Self-reflection, creativity**
Materials:	**Family photos, printer or scanner, brown paint, glue, green construction paper, scissors, butcher paper or poster board**
Number of Children:	**1+**
Where to Play:	**Inside**

BEFORE YOU START

★ Tell your children that today you'll be making a family art project that will help you remember your ancestors. Define the term "ancestor" for your child or children if they're not familiar with it. Try saying something like:

An ancestor is a family member who came before us. Usually, this means somebody from the distant past, like a great-great-great grandparent. When a family member dies, and we keep growing, they eventually become ancestors too. We get to take the things we inherited from them and carry them with us.

HOW TO PLAY

★ Place your butcher or poster paper on a flat surface. Ask your children to work together to paint a tree trunk and branches that takes up most of the page. You'll be adding leaves later, so make sure to leave enough blank space for them on the paper.

★ While the paint dries, look through your family photos together. Save or set aside at least one photo of each family member you find. Take special time when you come across photos of your recently deceased family member to talk about the memories their photos bring up.

★ Print copies of your selected photos and scan any hard copies if necessary. Make sure not to use any originals that can't be replaced.

(continued on next page)

* Cut leaves out of construction paper that are large enough to hold your family photos. Glue your photos to the leaves.
* Your children can work together to arrange the leaves on the branches of your tree. Place older or more distant relatives at the top of the tree and work your way down, making sure photos of your children are at the bottom.
* Once you're happy with how the tree looks, glue the leaves in place.
* Talk about any similarities you find between photos of different family members on your tree. Do you notice any physical traits in common? Does anybody share gestures, facial expressions, or body language with another person? Do any of your family members have similar senses of style?
* Point out any differences that you notice as well, such as differences in age, height, personality, and interests.

REFLECTION AND LEARNING QUESTIONS

* Based on this tree, what words would you use to describe our family?
* What traits do you think we have passed down most often?
* What did you inherit from our special person who died?
* What would you like to pass on to younger generations of our family?

Blended, foster, or adoptive families might want to depict an orchard instead of a single tree. You can emphasize traits your family members share that aren't genetic, such as hobbies and pet peeves. You can also wonder aloud about the many wonderful traits your child must have inherited from biological ancestors, whether or not they've had a chance to meet.

PARTS OF ME PORTRAIT

Finding similarities with a loved one is an important step in making meaning after loss. However, discovering what makes us unique can be just as important. A self-portrait allows children to reflect on how they would like to stay connected to their loved one while retaining their own identity.

Age Range:	**7–11**
Skills:	**Self-reflection, mindfulness, creativity**
Materials:	**Mirror, paper, colored pencils**
Number of Children:	**1**
Where to Play:	**Inside**

BEFORE YOU START

★ Talk with your child about personal qualities that they feel the proudest of. These can be physical attributes, personal strengths, personality traits, or special interests.

HOW TO PLAY

★ Set up your child where they can sit comfortably in front of a mirror to draw their self-portrait.

★ Encourage your child to stay mindful as they draw. Rather than drawing their face how they think it appears in their mind's eye, they can really notice and appreciate their reflection in front of them. Prompt your child to study their hair, the shape of their face, and their facial features.

★ Once your child has completed their drawing, ask if anything about their reflection or finished portrait surprised them. For example, do they appear more grown-up than they used to? Was your child's mental image of themselves still accurate, or have they changed?

★ Divide the background of the portrait into two halves by drawing a vertical line down the center of the page. Don't draw on the portrait itself.

★ On the left-hand side of the portrait, ask your child to write down the parts of themselves they have in common with their loved one. These can be traits, hobbies, talents, values, or interests they and their loved one shared.

(continued on next page)

* On the right-hand side, ask your child to write down the parts of themselves that are different from their loved one. These could include different tastes in music, movies, or food, interests that are unique to your child, or sources of disagreement between your child and their loved one.
* Ask your child to share their finished portrait with you.

REFLECTION AND LEARNING QUESTIONS

* Which of the traits you share with your loved one is most important to you?
* Which of your unique traits do you value the most?
* Is there anything your special person taught you or passed on to you that you're thankful for?
* Imagine you had made this portrait before our special person died. Do you think you would have written anything different?

Occasionally. children respond to grief by subconsciously trying to fill their loved one's shoes and taking on their characteristics. This may be especially likely after a sibling dies. Appreciating shared traits with a lost loved one is helpful. but this kind of emulating may not be. If you notice big changes in your child's interests. hobbies. or values after a death. consider bringing it up to a counselor.

WHAT'S YOUR SPARK?

Inspired by Pixar's movie *Soul,* this activity helps children name and think about the things in life that light them up inside. These small joys are part of what makes life worth living, and learning to notice and appreciate them can help children find more meaning in everyday life.

Age Range:	**8–11**
Skills:	**Self-reflection, creativity**
Materials:	**Wide-mouth glass jar, tissue paper, markers, Mod Podge, paintbrush, tea light (real or battery-operated)**
Number of Children:	**1+**
Where to Play:	**Inside**

BEFORE YOU START
★ It's helpful but not absolutely necessary to watch *Soul* before trying this activity. Older children may find the story very powerful, but it could be too abstract for younger kids to appreciate.

HOW TO PLAY
★ Talk with your children or child about the concept of a spark. If you've watched *Soul* together, you can reference the scenes in which characters tried to figure out their spark. Tell your child:

A spark is something that lights us up inside and makes us feel warm and happy. It's something we could do for hours and not notice that any time has passed. You don't have to be really good at it. It just needs to bring you joy and make the hours feel like seconds. Sparks are part of what make life worth living.

★ Talk with your child about what they imagine their spark could be. Remind them that you don't have to be particularly talented at something in order for it to be your spark. A child's spark could be a hobby, favorite activity, a subject they love learning about, a cause or passion, or anything that brings them a sense of joy.
★ If a child is able to list multiple sparks, that's great! There's no need to pick just one. In fact, sometimes it can be a lot of pressure for a child to feel like they have to choose one defining spark.

* Once your children have identified one or more sparks, ask them to write down some words or draw pictures on tissue paper to represent their chosen activity. If the spark is hard to define literally through words or pictures, tell them to jot down or sketch activities, moments, scenery, objects, animals, or people connected to the spark.
* Cut out your child's words and drawings from the tissue paper.
* Cut your remaining pieces of tissue paper into small squares or strips until you have enough paper to cover your glass jar. Be sure to include a variety of colors.
* Use Mod Podge and a paintbrush to help your child cover their jars with their words, drawings, and the blank strips of tissue paper. Continue until there's no bare glass remaining.
* Allow your jar to dry. Once it's finished, place the tea light inside to create a lantern.
* Light your candle and place your child's new lantern somewhere where it can remind them of their spark. Talk about the importance of doing things that "light us up" on a regular basis. Show your children how the one light inside of the lantern casts many shapes and colors on the outside. Likewise, a spark can inspire all parts of your life.

REFLECTION AND LEARNING QUESTIONS

* How do you feel when you are doing the activity you chose as your spark?
* Have you ever had the feeling of being so absorbed in an activity that you got lost in your own thoughts? What were you doing?
* At the end *Soul*, Joe says he is going to make sure to enjoy more of the small things in life. What are some small things you can enjoy?
* What do you think your special person's spark was?

SHOWING THANK YOU

Finding gratitude is an important part of meaning-making. However, pushing children to practice gratitude on a large scale may feel as though we're minimizing their grief. This activity instead focuses on identifying one person who has been helpful to your child during the grief process and finding a hands-on way to express thanks.

Age Range:	**8–11**
Skills:	**Gratitude, self-reflection**
Materials:	**Zoom or another video platform (if playing online)**
Number of Children:	**1+**
Where to Play:	**Inside, online**

BEFORE YOU START

★ Talk about the concept of gratitude with your children. You can define feeling gratitude as being thankful for things beyond presents and material possessions, that it's an everyday process of noticing and appreciating the big and small things in our lives that are good, helpful, or beautiful, even when life is very difficult.

★ Talk about the benefits of gratitude: It helps us feel better and makes others feel good too. Suggest that you take baby steps toward gratitude by finding just one person to thank, for something big or small. Younger children can appreciate the value of performing acts of kindness for others. Older children are capable of deeper empathy and may recognize the benefits of practicing gratitude that go beyond feeling good in the moment.

HOW TO PLAY

★ First, validate for your child or children that it can be really hard to feel grateful for anything after somebody dies. That's normal, understandable, and perfectly okay. Validate for your child that feeling ungrateful at the moment doesn't mean they are a bad person.

★ Think out loud about the people who were especially helpful during your grief process. This can include people who were involved in caring for your loved one before their death, such as doctors, nurses, home health aides, or hospice workers. Children might also wish to thank neighbors, friends, relatives, or other adults who helped to care for them or who provided emotional support after the death.

(continued on next page)

* Ask each child to choose one person to thank.
* Now think about the best way to thank this particular individual. Take their personality, wants, and needs into consideration to come up with an idea that feels special for that person. Some possibilities to consider:
  * Writing a thank-you letter or email
  * Baking cookies or another treat
  * Bringing a treat for the hospice staff where your loved one stayed
  * Calling on the phone to express your appreciation
  * Choosing a small gift to send
  * Paying their kindness forward to someone else, perhaps by helping another family in similar circumstances
* Help your child to carry out their plan. If you're playing online, stick with emails, phone calls, or gift giving, or tap another adult local to your child to assist.
* Encourage your child to notice how they feel before, during, and after showing their gratitude. Did they notice a shift in their mood?

REFLECTION AND LEARNING QUESTIONS

* What was it like to show your thanks, instead of just saying it to someone?
* How did your person react when you showed your gratitude? What do you think it was like for them?
* Can you think of anyone or anything else you are thankful for?
* How or why do you think gratitude can help people who are grieving?

LETTER TO MY PAST SELF

This activity helps your tween travel back in time to "talk" to the person they were immediately following their loved one's death. Letter writing gives kids an opportunity to practice positive, comforting self-talk.

Age Range:	8–11
Skills:	Self-reflection, communication
Materials:	Stationery and pen or word processor, Zoom or another video platform (if playing online)
Number of Children:	1
Where to Play:	Inside, online

BEFORE YOU START

★ Ask your child to take a moment and reflect on who they were and how they felt right after their loved one's death. What has changed since then?

HOW TO PLAY

★ Address this letter to your child's past self; for example: "9-year-old Sophie" or "Max in 2020."

★ Ask your child to imagine they could travel back in time to the days after their loved one's death. If they could write and deliver a letter, knowing what they know now, what would they say to help their past self through the pain of grief?

★ Encourage your child to write their letter in the present tense, like they would if they could really deliver it. If your child needs suggestions, here are some sentence stems they can complete to get started:

- Right now, you are feeling...
- You are wondering if...
- I want you to know that...
- Something that will help is...
- One way you will change is...
- Something to look forward to is...
- I'm proud of you for...
- Always remember that...

★ Ask your child if they would like to share their letter with you or keep it private. It can help to share these thoughts with others, but it's not absolutely necessary.

REFLECTION AND LEARNING QUESTIONS

★ How are you feeling after writing your letter?
★ Did you realize anything new while you were writing?

APPRECIATING FRAGILE THINGS

Philosophers have suggested that life is meaningful because it doesn't last forever. We tend to value things that are fragile because we appreciate that they may only be with us for a limited time. It's a heady concept for kids to grasp, but this activity makes it more concrete.

Age Range:	**9–11**
Skills:	**Emotional intelligence**
Materials:	**Fresh and artificial flowers, two vases**
Number of Children:	**1**
Where to Play:	**Inside**

BEFORE YOU START

* Reflect on how this concept fits into your child's or family's spiritual beliefs. This activity is based on the writings of Sallie Tisdale, a hospice nurse who writes from a Buddhist perspective, but it's not specific to any one belief system.

HOW TO PLAY

* Place your fresh flowers in a vase of water on the table. Set your artificial flowers and a second, empty vase nearby.
* Ask your child which they would rather get as a present: the fresh flowers or the artificial ones? Which of the two types of flowers would they be more likely to give to somebody else? Which one seems fanciest?
* Compare a few other items, such as a porcelain cup and a Styrofoam cup, a fresh piece of fruit and canned fruit, or a marble vase and a plastic vase. Which of these items seems the nicest, fanciest, or most expensive?
* After you've thought about it, share the following:

The fresh flowers or fruit, the porcelain cup, or the marble vase feel much more special to most people, even though the stuff made from plastic or Styrofoam is much sturdier. Isn't it funny that we love these breakable things? Even though the flowers and fruit will wither away, we still value them too.

* See if your child has any guesses about why the "fancy" versions of these items are more delicate. What are the benefits of a sturdy item? What are the drawbacks? Why do people spend more money on things that they have to handle with care?
* After your child has had a chance to make a few guesses, continue by saying:

Some people believe that when something isn't going to last forever, it helps us to value it more. It's special because it's only here for a short time. Life can be like that too. Nobody's life lasts forever, so every day is special and important.

* Ask your child to arrange the artificial flowers in the vase until they come up with a design they like.
* See if you can come up with any other life experiences that are more special or fun because they are time-limited, such as vacations, holidays, or visiting a special place. Would a vacation that never ended be as fun? What would it really be like if every day was your birthday?
* Keep your fresh flowers on display and enjoy them for the short time that they last. Put your artificial flowers somewhere where they can remind your child of their activity and what makes life valuable.

REFLECTION AND LEARNING QUESTIONS

* How was this activity for you?
* Can you think of other things that are valuable to us even though they last a short time?
* What can we do to remind ourselves that every day is special?

KINTSUGI, PART 1

We often talk about the negative effects of trauma and loss. Recently, however, therapists and researchers have become interested in the positive effects of overcoming hard times, called "post-traumatic growth." This activity uses *kintsugi*, the Japanese art of putting broken pottery pieces back together with gold, to explore how painful experiences can also lead to resilience.

Age Range:	10–11
Skills:	Self-reflection, creativity
Materials:	Broken pot or dish or a thrift store dish with a heavy ziplock bag, ceramic glue, gold-toned paint, small paintbrush
Number of Children:	1
Where to Play:	Inside, outside

BEFORE YOU START

★ This activity requires handling broken dishes, so adult supervision is required. Choose a time to play when you're able to directly supervise and find an appropriate workspace.

HOW TO PLAY

★ If you happen to have a broken dish at home, you are ready to begin. Otherwise, take your inexpensive dish and place it inside the ziplock bag. Use a mallet or hard surface to break the dish into a few large pieces. For safety reasons, make sure this step is done by an adult.

★ If you'd like, you and your child can search online for images of *kintsugi* pottery for inspiration as you explain the concept. To introduce this activity to your child, read the following or put it into your own words:

Today we are going to try out a special kind of Japanese art called "kintsugi." Kintsugi means "to join with gold." When a piece of pottery breaks, instead of throwing it away, kintsugi artists fill the broken places with gold to put it back together again. They believe that when something breaks and is repaired, it becomes more beautiful because it now has a unique story.

* Have your child dip the paintbrush into the ceramic glue and paint the glue onto the edges of the broken pot. Older children can often do this independently, maybe with some assistance from an adult to first get the pieces in order.
* Let the glue dry. Once it's dry, have your child dip the paintbrush into the gold paint and gently trace over the cracks to highlight them.
* Admire your new work of art with your child. Tell them that just like some objects become stronger after breaking, people can also grow and become stronger after things fall apart in their lives.
* Reflect on the ways you and your child have changed for the better since your loved one's death. For example, perhaps you have more empathy for others, or you have more appreciation for the good things in life.
* Find a special place to put your *kintsugi* art on display.

REFLECTION AND LEARNING QUESTIONS
* What do you think about *kintsugi*?
* What does this piece of art make you think of when you look at it?
* How does this piece of art make you feel?
* Can you think of other things we could fix when they break, instead of throwing them away?
* How might keeping and fixing them make those items more special?

When talking about growth after loss, we want to be careful not to minimize any negative feelings a child might have. Death is sad and unfair, *and* dealing with it can also help us become stronger, more resilient people.

KINTSUGI, PART 2

If you're working with young children or don't want to deal with broken dishes, this variation of the *Kintsugi* activity uses construction paper to explore similar ideas about growth after loss.

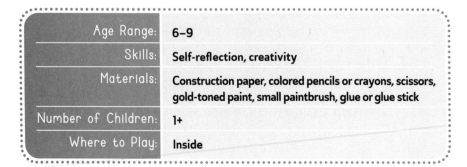

Age Range:	6–9
Skills:	Self-reflection, creativity
Materials:	Construction paper, colored pencils or crayons, scissors, gold-toned paint, small paintbrush, glue or glue stick
Number of Children:	1+
Where to Play:	Inside

BEFORE YOU START

* Choose one color of construction paper to use as your background, and another to represent your pottery.
* Show your child pictures of *kintsugi* art online. Explain that this very old form of Japanese art puts broken pieces back together again using gold. Let them know that today you'll be trying out something a little like *kintsugi* at home.

HOW TO PLAY

* Ask your children how they would feel if they broke something fancy, like a vase. Sad? Frustrated? Embarrassed?
* Tell your children that some people believe that things that are broken become more beautiful and precious than they were before, because now they have a story to tell.
* Trace a vase shape onto your pottery paper with a pencil. Repeat as many vase shapes as needed for the number of children participating. Each child will need one vase. Cut out your vases.
* Trace the vase shape onto your background paper as well, to make assembly easier later. Each child will need one background paper.
* Give each child a paper "vase." They can decorate their vase however they wish with the crayons or pencils.
* Once the children have finished, ask your children to rip their vases into a few large pieces so they look like broken pottery.

* Using glue or a glue stick, arrange the pieces of paper onto a sheet of the background color to re-create the shape of the vase.
* Help each child fill in the cracks between pieces with their gold paint. Show off your finished *kintsugi* art!

REFLECTION AND LEARNING QUESTIONS

* What do you think about *kintsugi*?
* Have you ever broken something that was special to you?
* Can you think of a way you have grown or changed since our loved one died?

CHAPTER 11

LOOKING TO THE FUTURE

Most of the activity chapters in this book have focused on the death of your child's loved one: sharing memories, sorting out feelings, and understanding the impact of the loss. This chapter is a little bit different. As children work through their grief, they need to eventually find a way to keep moving forward in life. How can children hold on to their loved one's memory without feeling stuck in their grief?

The activities in this chapter help children and families find each other again after a loss, and figure out who they'd like to become. They encourage children to start imagining a future that includes new experiences and feelings besides grief. You'll find activities that promote family bonding, explore the idea of growing up, and help kids identify new things to look forward to. This kind of thinking instills hope in children and reduces their risk of depression.

These activities aren't intended to push kids to "move on from" or "forget about" grief. Instead, they're about balance. Grief is a lifelong process, and over time children and caregivers can learn to hold their memories of a loved one in their hearts while continuing to adjust to a new and different world.

THEMED FAMILY PORTRAIT

This fun twist on family portraits helps younger children express their sense of identity and belonging. Even without words, you can learn a lot about how your child views themselves and others based on how they depict their family members.

Age Range:	**5–7**
Skills:	**Creativity, imagination, self-reflection**
Materials:	**Paper; crayons, markers, or colored pencils; Zoom or another video platform (if playing online)**
Number of Children:	**1**
Where to Play:	**Inside, online**

BEFORE YOU START

★ Have a conversation about families and all the different ways they can look. *Families Can* by Dan Saks and *The Family Book* by Todd Parr are good options.

HOW TO PLAY

★ Challenge your child to draw a picture of your whole family. There's only one catch: the family members can't just be drawn as themselves. Instead, your child will represent everyone in the family using symbols, characters, or animals.

★ If your child needs some inspiration, consider drawing the family as emojis, superheroes, animals, cartoon characters, or mythical creatures.

★ Encourage your child to be creative and use their imagination with this picture. It's okay for it to be silly! They can also include pets or other important non-family members.

★ Your child can draw their picture on paper, or if you're playing together online, they might prefer to use the whiteboard function on your platform.

★ Ask your child if they'd like you to watch them as they work, or if you should be surprised by their drawing at the end.

★ Your child can discuss their finished portrait with you and explain their choices, as well as share it with any other available family members.

REFLECTION AND LEARNING QUESTIONS

★ Why did you pick this theme?
★ How did you decide how to draw each person in our family?
★ What makes our family unique?

PAPER BAG PUPPET SHOW

Families can feel fractured after a significant person dies. Playful, collaborative activities like this one reinforce a family's sense of cohesion. Connected families increase children's sense of felt safety, bolstering them as they continue to process grief.

Age Range:	**5–10**
Skills:	**Creativity**
Materials:	**Paper bags, glue, felt, construction paper, pom-poms, googly eyes, a phone (for recording)**
Number of Children:	**1+**
Where to Play:	**Inside**

BEFORE YOU START

★ This activity works best in larger groups, and children may appreciate an audience for their performance.

HOW TO PLAY

★ Lay your paper bags flat on your table or work surface. Turn each bag upside down so that the opening is at the bottom and the creased flap is at the top.

★ Create a face for your puppet by adding eyes and a nose to the flat, creased bottom of the bag. The top half of the mouth should run along the bottom edge of the flap, with the bottom half of the mouth finishing just below the flap.

★ Have each family member design their own puppet, using whatever materials they like to create the face and body.

★ Work together as a group to create and rehearse a story to perform with your puppets. The story should have a beginning, middle, and end, and include an opportunity for all puppets to speak.

★ If you have a hard time coming up with ideas, consider using a fairy tale such as "Little Red Riding Hood," "Hansel and Gretel," or "The Three Little Pigs" as a starting point. As a family, invent a new ending to the story.

★ Once you've created your puppet show, it's time to perform! You can act out your story for a live audience or record it on video for children to watch afterward.

REFLECTION AND LEARNING QUESTIONS

★ How did our family do with working together as a team?
★ What did you contribute to our performance that you're proud of?

TRAVEL PASSPORT

Traveling to new places is a pleasurable, mood-boosting activity—and it's also a good metaphor for the journey grieving kids go on as they adapt to life without their loved one. Help your child think about new possible sources of joy by setting travel goals, both big and small.

Age Range:	**5–11**
Skills:	**Creativity, imagination**
Materials:	**Blue and white construction paper, markers, stapler, rubber stamp**
Number of Children:	**1**
Where to Play:	**Inside**

BEFORE YOU START
* Ensure that younger children understand what a passport is and what it does. Try saying something like "A passport is a special little book that shows where we come from and keeps track of all the places where we travel."

HOW TO PLAY
* Fold two pieces of white paper and one piece of blue paper in half widthwise.
* Place your two folded white sheets inside your folded blue sheet, with your folded edges facing the same direction. This should create an eight-page booklet with a blue front and back cover. Add staples along the binding to create your passport.
* Your child can begin by decorating the front and back covers of their passport. They can use a real passport for inspiration or create their own design.
* The first interior page is for your child's identifying information to make their passport "official." They can draw a picture of themselves here and include their name, birthdate, and address.
* On the second page, your child can write and draw about their hometown.
* On the third page, ask your child to write or draw about a place they have visited in the past and enjoyed.

(continued on next page)

* The following pages are for places your child would like to visit someday. Think about locations both near and far, starting close to home and moving farther away. As an example:
  * Page four: a place to visit in the neighborhood
  * Page five: a place to visit in my city or town
  * Page six: a place to visit in my state
  * Page seven: a place to visit in my country
  * Page eight: a place to visit anywhere in the world
* Once your child has finished their writing and drawing, get out your rubber stamp. Explain that each time you visit a new place, you get to add a stamp to your passport. Your child can go ahead and add a stamp to pages two and three!
* Make a plan to visit one of the unstamped places in the passport. Set a date for the visit and put it on the calendar.

REFLECTION AND LEARNING QUESTIONS

* People live differently all over the world. What do you imagine is the same or different in the places you'd like to visit?
* Which place would you be most excited to visit?
* Can you think about any challenges you might encounter trying to travel there?
* Sometimes people describe grief as a journey. What do you think they mean when they say that?

If traveling far isn't a possibility for you right now. It's okay to choose more destinations that are closer to home. It's also okay to remind your child that faraway places are a "someday" goal. not something to do right now. What's most important is that you imagine new. exciting. different experiences to try together.

FAMILY FLAG

Families can come together after a loss to redefine who they are as a team and remind each other of what's most important. This collaborative art activity encourages family members to create a new symbol to represent their family and values.

Age Range:	**5–11**
Skills:	**Creativity, cooperation**
Materials:	**Large piece of felt and assorted smaller felt pieces, fabric glue, fabric scissors, puffy paint, wooden dowel or stick**
Number of Children:	**2+**
Where to Play:	**Inside**

BEFORE YOU START
★ Flip through some family albums before starting this activity. That way, important family milestones will be fresh on everyone's mind.

HOW TO PLAY
★ Your job as a family will be to design a flag that everyone feels good about as a representation of your family.
★ Select one color to represent each member of your family. Use all of these colors to create a design or pattern for the background of your flag.
★ Choose a symbol to represent your family and provide a focal point for your flag. Animals, plants, or celestial images like the sun, moon, or stars can be a great choice.
★ Finally, add any extra decorations to your flag to represent important family values or favorite activities, vacations, or memories.
★ You may want to sketch out your ideas in advance. Once you've finalized your plan, cut shapes out of your smaller felt pieces to glue to your large piece, which will form the base of your flag. Use puffy paint for additional details.
★ Once your flag has dried, glue the large felt base to your dowel, and your work is complete!

REFLECTION AND LEARNING QUESTIONS
★ Where should we hang our family flag?
★ If we had a family motto, what would it be?

THREE MAGIC WISHES

Imagining new ways to find joy is an important part of moving forward after loss. By identifying three wishes they'd like to have granted, kids can begin to discover ways to find new happiness for themselves.

Age Range:	**5–11**
Skills:	**Imagination**
Materials:	**Paper, art supplies, Zoom or another video platform (if playing online)**
Number of Children:	**1**
Where to Play:	**Inside, online**

BEFORE YOU START
* Tell your child you'd like to imagine what it would be like to have a magic wand or a genie that has the power to grant a person wishes.

HOW TO PLAY
* Tell your child:

  Imagine that you have a lamp with a genie inside who has the power to let you do any three things that your heart desires. The genie can't change the past; you can only make things happen in the present or future. If you had three wishes to do anything you wanted, what would you wish for?

* Ask your child to draw their three wishes for you, either using paper and art supplies or a digital whiteboard function or screenshare. Encourage them to include as much detail as possible to make the wishes seem real.
* Review your child's drawings. Ask Reflection and Learning Questions to identify any themes from the pictures that could inspire real-life activities. For example, you may not be able to go scuba diving with a giant squid, but you might be able to visit the aquarium, plan a trip to a beach, or set up a fish tank at home.

REFLECTION AND LEARNING QUESTIONS
* Can you think of small ways we could make these wishes come true in real life?
* What kind of activities could we try that might get you closer to your wish?
* What places could we visit together that might remind you a bit of your wish?

FAMILY HOPE CHAIN

Help family members of all ages express their hopes, dreams, and wishes for the future with this simple craft project. Appropriate for all ages, linking each family member's contributions together to form a chain represents unity and strength.

Age Range:	5–11
Skills:	Self-reflection, cooperation
Materials:	Different colors of construction paper, cellophane tape, scissors, pencils and crayons
Number of Children:	2+
Where to Play:	Inside

BEFORE YOU START
★ This activity works best with slightly larger groups, so you may wish to recruit extra adults to play.

HOW TO PLAY
★ Cut rectangular strips of construction paper measuring roughly 2 inches by 8 inches. Be sure to include a variety of colors.
★ Continue until you have cut three to five strips for each participating player. Distribute your paper strips evenly among all players in your group.
★ Invite all family members to write or draw their future hopes, wishes, and dreams for themselves and the family. These can be big or small, realistic or fantastic. There are no right or wrong wishes to have.
★ Taking turns, share one wish at a time with the rest of the group.
★ As each player reads their wish aloud, help them tape the two ends of the strip together to form a loop.

REFLECTION AND LEARNING QUESTIONS
★ Did anybody else come up with a wish that you liked too?
★ Did anybody have the same or similar wishes?
★ Chains are strong and tough. Can you think of ways our family has been strong or tough?
★ Are there any small steps we can take to make some of these hopes come true?
★ Where should we put our chain so the whole family can see it?

NEW FAMILY TRADITION

Often, the death of a loved one means that family life doesn't look and feel the way it used to. Old traditions may not feel right anymore in the "new normal." Creating a new family tradition together is a chance to reconnect and envision a future that, while different, still includes moments of happiness and celebration.

Age Range:	5–11
Skills:	Imagination, cooperation
Materials:	None
Number of Children:	1+
Where to Play:	Inside

BEFORE YOU START

★ Think about your family's current needs and what kind of tradition you'd like to create in order to meet them. You may want to consider how your family dynamics have changed after your loss, and how a new tradition could help bridge a gap. For example, you may be looking for a different way to celebrate a holiday or an opportunity for family togetherness and bonding now that schedules have changed.

HOW TO PLAY

★ Once you have decided what function you'd like your new tradition to serve, daydream with your children about possibilities for your new tradition.

★ If you're trying to come up with a tradition to help you adapt to a specific change, such as a new place to celebrate a holiday now that you won't be visiting your loved one, let your children know your thoughts. Ask if they agree that a new tradition could help and see if they have any ideas about what they will need around that time.

★ It's also okay for your goals for this tradition to be more open-ended, such as finding a way to just have fun and be together at a regularly scheduled time.

★ Choose an activity to form the basis of your new tradition. Any activity that is joyful or personally meaningful can be the basis for a new tradition. As you brainstorm with your family, consider the following options:
  • Pastimes or activities the entire family enjoys
  • Songs, food, or rituals that connect you to your culture or ancestors' culture

- Hobbies or outings that will let the family spend time together in a new or different way
- Books, songs, or movies that your family loves or finds comforting

★ Traditions help families share what is important to them. Think about any family values that you'd like to express through your new tradition, such as generosity, gratitude, learning, or kindness. How might you show or include these values in your tradition?

★ Decide when this new tradition should occur. For example, on a holiday or on one Saturday every month. Having some structure helps a tradition feel special and important, but there's no need to be overly rigid in determining a time.

★ If relevant, choose a place for this tradition to occur, such as the family dinner table or a special place your family loves to visit.

★ Give all family members a chance to share their opinions and fine-tune your new tradition. Everybody should have a chance to contribute ideas so that the finished tradition feels like it belongs to everyone. Keep tinkering with your plan until all participants feel they have reached a good compromise.

★ Plan on a date to enjoy your tradition together for the first time. Mark it on the phone or on a calendar to provide a visual reminder.

REFLECTION AND LEARNING QUESTIONS

★ What do you think about our new tradition?

★ How does it feel to try something different?

★ Can you think of other times that we might want to try doing something new as a family?

You or your children may want to build an acknowledgment of your loved one into your tradition, especially if the tradition will occur at a time you used to spend together. It is always okay to do this if it feels right for your family. Find ways to help your children reconnect and enjoy time spent together as a family unit, even as you acknowledge and remember your grief.

GROWING UP PORTRAITS

Something wonderful about kids is that they are always growing and changing. Even when something terrible happens, they can't help but make strides forward. It can be fun to imagine with your child what they might be like years into the future.

Age Range:	7–11
Skills:	Imagination, self-reflection, creativity
Materials:	Paper, colored pencils, or markers; Zoom or another video platform (if playing online)
Number of Children:	1
Where to Play:	Inside, online

BEFORE YOU START

★ Daydream with your child about who they will grow up to be. Where will they live? How will they dress? What will they be doing with their time?

HOW TO PLAY

★ Ask your child to draw three self-portraits envisioning themselves five, ten, and twenty years into the future.
★ These pictures can include goals your child is working toward, like a dream school or job, but if your child hasn't thought that far ahead yet, that's okay too. They can just daydream for today, and know that their answers could change tomorrow.
★ Your child can add any extra details they choose, including backgrounds, friends, pets, cars, or anything else they feel is important.
★ Once your child has finished all three drawings, ask them to present the pictures to you, explaining what they've chosen to depict.
★ Ask questions to improve your own understanding of the drawings, as well as to help your child envision the future they've imagined for themselves in clearer detail.

REFLECTION AND LEARNING QUESTIONS

★ Which of these ages is your favorite, and why?
★ What kind of job do you imagine you might work someday?
★ Do you think you will have kids of your own? Why or why not?
★ What do you think will still be the same about you?
★ What do you think will be the most different thing about future you?

PERSONAL COAT OF ARMS

Coats of arms let knights and nobles identify themselves without speaking a word. The symbols used on a coat of arms represented important aspects of who a person was and where they came from. This art project helps kids declare their identity to the world, as they see it.

Age Range:	**8–11**
Skills:	**Creativity, self-reflection**
Materials:	**Large piece of cardboard, scissors, markers or paint**
Number of Children:	**1**
Where to Play:	**Inside**

BEFORE YOU START
★ Show your child a few examples of coats of arms for inspiration before starting this activity. Most coats of arms resemble a large shield.

HOW TO PLAY
★ Cut your cardboard into a large shield shape.
★ Draw perpendicular lines across your shield to divide it into four quarters.
★ Invite your child to decorate their coat of arms using any colors they'd like, featuring one symbol on each of the four sections.
★ The symbols on a coat of arms often represented accomplishments the individual or their family took pride in and wanted others to know about. Your child might also want to consider using their favorite animal or finding a symbol to represent their favorite hobby or the place their family is from.
★ For a little extra fun, ask your child to create a motto to go along with their coat of arms. This could be a favorite quote or a saying they feel expresses their personality. You can write this on the bottom of the crest or use some scrap cardboard to create a plaque to attach below it.

REFLECTION AND LEARNING QUESTIONS
★ What symbols did you put on your crest, and why?
★ What is something you've done that you are the proudest of?
★ What is something that makes you proud of our family?

ON THIS DAY...

Most social media–savvy kids are familiar with the nostalgic "On This Day" function offered on Facebook, Instagram, and the Apple Photos app. We can use this familiar format to reflect on everyday moments from the past and imagine what slices of life your child will create in the years to come.

Age Range:	**8–11**
Skills:	**Imagination, creativity**
Materials:	**Smartphone, tablet, or computer; Zoom or another video platform (if playing online)**
Number of Children:	**1**
Where to Play:	**Inside, online**

BEFORE YOU START

★ Select an age-appropriate app that has enough photos of your child stored on it to complete this activity. Be mindful about the timing of when you introduce this exercise: It might be difficult for children to encounter unexpected images of their loved one, or to reflect on holidays or major milestones.

HOW TO PLAY

★ Access the "Memories" or "On This Day" function on your app of choice.
★ See how far back your memories go and talk about them with your child. How old is your child in the earliest picture?
★ Ask your child what they remember about these days in the past. Did they seem important at the time?
★ Use Apple Photos or a similar app to create a slideshow of the photos you've found. Your child can decide which memories to include and select music to accompany them. Talk about how it feels to see all these everyday photos turned into a special presentation. Does it make those moments feel different or more important?
★ Next, imagine that you are one, five, or even ten years in the future. What kind of pictures might come up in your "On This Day" memories?
★ Ask your child to search online for photos to represent what they imagine will pop up on their phones at each of these points in the future. Think about the kind of events your child will want to commemorate with a photo in the coming years. For example:

- Someone in a cap and gown, to represent graduating from high school
- An animal, to represent a future pet
- Pictures of a business that could be a possible first job
- A beach, movie theater, or other location where your child could have fun with friends or family
- Car keys or pictures of a dream car to represent learning to drive

★ Ask your child to share their chosen photos with you, either in person or by sharing their screen.

REFLECTION AND LEARNING QUESTIONS

★ What is it like to imagine your life so far in the future?

★ What sort of everyday moments do you hope to have more of in the future?

★ What moments do you hope to have fewer of?

★ Can you think of anything about daily life we usually take for granted but is actually really fun or special?

LIFELINE MOBILE

The lifeline is a classic therapy activity that lets children reflect on past experiences while also dreaming of the future. It's helpful for grieving kids because it helps to put difficult experiences into context. I've added a second step to encourage children to further visualize their hopes for the future.

Age Range:	10+
Skills:	Imagination
Materials:	White paper, colored pencils, scissors, hole punch, coat hanger, string
Number of Children:	1
Where to Play:	Inside

BEFORE YOU START

★ This activity requires some facilitation by a grownup. Introduce the activity to your child by saying something like "Today I want us to try making a time line of your life. You can include anything you want on it that was important to you, good or bad."

HOW TO PLAY

★ Draw a horizontal line across a sheet of white paper, with two perpendicular, vertical lines on either end of the line. The line on the far left will be the start of your lifeline. Label this point with the year your child was born. The line on the far right will represent the present day, and you can label it accordingly.

★ Starting in early childhood and moving toward the present day, ask your child to brainstorm the most significant events in their life so far. Make additional vertical lines to mark where these events would fall on the time line of your child's life.

★ Ask about events occurring at certain ages if you notice big gaps in the time line. You can remind your child of the timing of major milestones like moves, new births in the family, or the addition of a pet. Ultimately, it's up to your child to decide what to include.

★ Keep going until the time line feels complete. At least five events would be a good goal to aim for.

★ Once you've finished, take out a second piece of paper, and draw new horizontal and vertical lines. Tell your child: "Now, let's take this time line into the future. I want you to tell me what you hope to do with your life, starting now and going forward until you are eighty or ninety years old."

★ Help your child brainstorm and move decade by decade along the time line, thinking about things such as career, family, personal goals, travel, and hobbies.

★ You can ask your child questions to help them visualize the distant future. For example, when does your child imagine they'll move into their own place? What do they think about having children someday? Where does your child see themselves at your age? How do they think they'll spend their retirement?

★ Take a moment to look at the time line together. This midpoint may be a good time to discuss some of the following Reflection and Learning Questions, or you can wait until the end if you prefer.

★ Have your child pick at least five events from their future time line to use for the second part of this activity. Draw pictures to represent these future moments on a fresh sheet of paper. These illustrations should be fairly small—about 3–5 inches is a good goal.

★ Use these illustrations to create a mobile of your child's most exciting hopes for the future. Cut the drawings out and punch a hole in each one. Use varying lengths of string to arrange the pictures and hang them from the coat hanger.

★ You and your child can select a place to hang this new mobile where they can look at it and be reminded of what they dreamed up.

REFLECTION AND LEARNING QUESTIONS

★ How does it feel to look at the whole story of your life like this?

★ Which past events on your time line were the happiest for you?

★ Which past events on your time line were the most difficult?

★ Is there anything about your time line you wish you could change?

★ What are you most excited about from your future time line?

★ What have you learned from your past that can help you achieve your future dreams?

APPLYING LESSONS TO DAILY LIFE

In Part 2, you learned a variety of hands-on ways to help your child manage grief. Some activities, like relaxation exercises, are intended for use again and again. Others, like the more labor-intensive craft projects, are one-time experiences. Just because an activity is finished, however, doesn't mean the lesson has to stop.

As your child enters their "new normal" after loss, they may find different ways to grieve. You may not need to open this book as often or lead your child in direct activities in the ways that we've practiced here. Over time, your child will learn how to carry a piece of their loved one inside their heart while also carrying on with the tasks of daily life.

This final part of the book will help you apply everything you've learned in the previous chapters to the next phase of your child's or family's life. Rather than setting aside specific times for activities, you can find simple ways to integrate small bits and pieces of the skills you've learned into your day-to-day interactions with your child.

Doing a single activity together is wonderful, but everyday moments are where the most growth and change can happen. Talking about your loved one, using coping skills, and spending quality time together become habits your child can rely on during times of stress. By continuing to practice the skills you've learned now, you are laying the groundwork for emotional well-being over the long run.

Your child's feelings about their loss will evolve and change over time. As your child matures, so will their understanding of grief. Before we close the chapter, we'll talk about how you can ensure that your child is continuing to process their grief in a healthy way, and when you should consider getting outside help.

CHAPTER 12

WHAT'S NEXT?

Grief never ends, but it can change. As time moves on, you may find that you and your child speak about your loss less often. You may notice changes in your child, such as fewer tears or a renewed interest in school and activities. You may find yourself wondering what to do next—has your child moved on? Should you still keep talking about grief if your child isn't?

On the other hand, as time goes by your child's emotions may surprise you. Whether it's problems at school, a deep depression, or anger at home, it can be hard to tell whether problems are just due to growing up or if they might be grief-related. How can you tell the difference, and when should you get help?

In this final chapter, we'll talk about the ways that a child's grief can change in the first few years following a death. You'll learn ways to carry the lessons of this book into your daily routine. We'll discuss common problems that arise for bereaved children as they grow, and what you can do to help. By the end of this chapter, you'll know how to support your child, how to identify warning signs of bigger problems, and when to seek therapy.

GRIEF IS A LIFELONG PROCESS

You've reached the end of this book, but this isn't the end of your child's grief story. The death of a significant person changes the course of a child's life. Mourning is never truly over. As your child grows, the effects of their loss will show up in new and potentially surprising ways.

As caregivers, we often want nothing more than to help our children avoid pain. We hope we can move them past it, help them forget it, or shift them back to the way they used to be. Of course, this isn't possible with grief. We can find new ways to move forward, but there's no going back.

This can be hard and painful to think about. As a possible reframe, consider that grief is the remaining love from your child's relationship with their special person. The impact of that loving relationship will last a lifetime, which means the grief will too.

CHILDREN REVISIT GRIEF AS THEY GROW

Although your child may appear to have worked through their feelings of grief for now, this may not be the case as they mature. As children grow up, their newfound understanding of death will allow them to grieve and process their loss in ways they weren't able to when they were younger.

If you think back to the first chapter of this book, you'll remember that children around the ages of three and four don't fully understand the finality of death and aren't able to think about it in an abstract way. As your child gets older, the reality of their permanent loss will become clearer. Children may start to think about their future and realize all the milestones their loved one will miss. This can be especially hard when non-bereaved peers aren't having to deal with the same pain.

If you notice your child re-grieving in this way. It doesn't mean something has gone wrong. or that your child is taking steps backward in their grief process. Your child may need some extra support as they revisit new and old feelings. but maturing in this way is healthy and helpful.

WHAT SITUATIONS CAN BE TRIGGERING FOR BEREAVED CHILDREN?

Some events are particularly tough for bereaved children, even in the long term. You can help your child prepare for difficult situations and strategize about how to cope with strong feelings about them. It's perfectly okay to modify activities as needed, or even skip some events altogether for a while if they're too painful to tolerate.

Keep an eye out for the following scenarios, which have the potential to trigger bereaved kids:

* Holidays
* Family reunions, weddings, or gatherings
* Spending time with non-bereaved peers' families
* The anniversary of the death, as well as other meaningful dates, such as their birthday, diagnosis, hospitalization, or funeral
* Other losses, such as the death of a pet or a move to a new house

It's not uncommon for grievers of all ages to have a difficult time around the anniversary of the death—even if the event isn't consciously on their mind.

You may also notice that your child has a larger than expected response to other losses. because each additional loss brings back feelings and memories from the first one. Being sensitive to these triggers can help you better understand your child's behavior and connect it back to their grief.

HOW TO SUPPORT YOUR CHILD OVER TIME

The same factors that promote resilience in the face of loss will also help your child in the future. All children benefit from having this kind of support, but it's especially critical for bereaved kids:

* A stable family system
* Consistent routines
* Attentive adults
* Healthy coping skills
* Ongoing opportunities to talk about and remember their loved one

The activities in this book can be an ongoing resource for all these skills, but it's not necessary to crack it open every time you'd like to support your child. Instead, you can weave these elements into your daily life in small, subtle ways. Let's take a look at three main things to keep in mind as your child grows: being mindful of changing family roles, integrating coping skills into daily life, and taking the initiative in talking about your loved one.

BE MINDFUL OF CHANGING FAMILY ROLES

We talked about maintaining consistent routines in the immediate aftermath of a loss, but what does that look like over the long term? As time goes on, things will understandably evolve in a family. Kids grow, activities change, and the routines that used to work won't be realistic forever.

However, family roles will also shift as you adjust to the death, especially if you have lost a primary caregiver like a parent or grandparent. Sometimes, bereaved kids wind up taking on too many responsibilities and may even start to fill the role of an extra adult in the house. These children don't get the time they need to just enjoy being a kid, and it can lead to resentment and behavior problems as they grow.

You can be mindful of this and keep family roles consistent by asking yourself questions such as:

* Does my child get free, unstructured time every day?
* Does my child have significantly more chores than other kids of the same age?
* Do I talk with my child about grown-up problems?
* Is my child overly worried about my feelings or their siblings' feelings?
* Does my older child act like a parent toward younger siblings?
* Does my child appear overwhelmed?
* Has my child started acting bossy with family, or are they giving advice on how to handle adult situations?

Not all families have the luxury of having outside help or a large support system following a death, so some changes in family responsibilities may be inevitable. By remaining mindful, you can help your child keep a sense of balance even as the family changes.

Sometimes, family roles shift in big ways that make children feel like they need to be caregivers for their siblings, or even for a surviving parent. Therapists call this "parentification." Parentified children need help to relearn appropriate boundaries so they can enjoy healthy relationships without feeling like they have to be a helper.

INTEGRATE COPING SKILLS INTO DAILY LIFE

In Chapters 5–7, you and your child learned skills for managing feelings of worry, anger, and sadness. Many of the skills your child has practiced in this book are adapted from techniques originally created for adults. There is no age limit on practicing deep breathing, spotting unhelpful thoughts, or journaling. Although we've introduced them in a playful way, the hope is that these skills can grow along with your child.

Learning emotion-regulation skills at an early age equips children with tools they can use to handle strong emotions for a lifetime. Trying a new coping skill for the first time might feel a little clunky or awkward, but with continued practice things start to feel easier. By continuing to model and reference coping skills, you can help them become a habit. Over time, these small actions can make a big difference in how your child copes with stress.

It's normal for children to gravitate toward a few skills that work well for them and discard the rest. It's okay if your child doesn't practice their skills exactly to the letter of this book, either. What's most important is that they've found a system that works for them.

You can integrate these skills into your day-to-day life in the following ways:

★ Name and empathize with your child's feelings: "I can see how that could make you angry."
★ Help your child notice overly negative thoughts by asking if there's any proof their worry could be true.

* Rather than prescribing a coping skill, offer choices to your child and let them choose a skill.
* Consider adding a relaxation practice into your daily routine, such as an after-dinner walk or a guided visualization before bed.
* Prioritize social, creative, and rewarding activities, especially during times of stress.
* Create opportunities for sensory play, which helps children stay mindful and grounded.
* Show your children that you can use these skills to self-regulate too.

TAKE THE INITIATIVE IN TALKING ABOUT YOUR LOVED ONE

In the beginning, your child likely had lots of opportunities to talk about their loved one. Whether at the funeral, with a school counselor, or with friends and family, children usually receive more sensitivity from people immediately following the death. As time goes on, these conversations happen less and less. Kids may pick up on an unspoken pressure to "move on," which may be imagined but might also contain a grain of truth.

It might be harder for you to speak about your loved one too. Parents and caregivers may see their child feeling better and wonder if they still need to talk about what happened. They might even worry that continuing to discuss their child's special person could lead to further pain.

Chances are good that even if your child isn't speaking about their loved one, they're still thinking about them. Just as you've watched your child grieve, they've witnessed your grief too. Children may avoid bringing up their loved one in an attempt to protect your feelings. This is especially true if you aren't mentioning them yourself, which kids may interpret as a sign that you don't want to talk.

Rather than waiting for your child to say something, it's okay to take the lead on these talks. As the grownup, your child is looking to you for clues about what's okay to discuss. It's not necessary to continue to do in-depth storytelling and sharing like we did in Chapter 8 forever—that's a lot of work!

Instead, you can show your child that you're still thinking about your loved one, and it's okay if they are too. One way to do this is by simply speaking your internal thoughts about your loved one aloud as they happen in day-to-day life. Consider sharing comments such as:

* "I remember the first time we went fishing here, you caught your first fish with Grandpa."
* "Dad would really have thought that movie was funny."
* "I was just thinking about Aunt Amy this morning, and wishing she could be here."

These don't need to be deep thoughts, and it's fine for you to let them arise naturally, rather than feeling forced to share things on a regular basis.

Another way to keep communication open is to "wonder aloud" about your child's experiences and feelings. This is a skill that child therapists often use, and it's one you can employ as a caregiver too.

We never know exactly what another person is thinking about, but you're an adult who knows your bereaved child extremely well. You know their history and have gone through this experience with them. You can help your child develop their awareness of their own feelings by sharing educated guesses.

Rather than putting words in your child's mouth, wondering aloud lets us draw a child's attention to a possible connection to their grief experience. You can make a statement like:

* "I can see that you really don't want to go on this trip, and I wonder if it's because the last time we went, Grandma was with us."
* "I've noticed you seem very sad this week, and I am remembering that this is the week last year that we first learned about Mom's cancer diagnosis."
* "It's so sad that our hamster died. I wonder if you're thinking about other times someone you love has died too."

Wondering aloud doesn't require a response from your child. It's perfectly fine if they agree or disagree with your suggestion. Either way, you're helping them make possible connections to their grief and reinforcing the idea that it's okay to talk about it.

WHAT IF MY CHILD NEEDS MORE HELP?

According to the Harvard Child Bereavement Study, which we discussed in Chapter 1, about one-third of children who suffer a loss will end up needing the help of a mental health professional. Because so many factors influence how a child adapts, it's possible that even with a very supportive environment, a child may struggle to bounce back from grief. Depression, anxiety, and other mental health problems are an understandable response to trauma and loss, not a sign that you or anyone else has done something wrong.

Keep in mind that the mental health problems associated with grief may not show up right away. Symptoms can emerge anywhere from several months to several years after the death. The more time that has elapsed since a trauma or stressful event occurred, the less specific the mental health problems tend to be. This can make it a little trickier to spot grief-related symptoms when they come up later.

Caregivers who are not aware of the ongoing impact of grief might mistakenly assume a child is simply struggling in school or being rebellious, when in reality a child's problems are tied to a loss that occurred years before. Keeping your child's history in mind and knowing what to look for will allow you to notice warning signs quickly and get your child the help they need.

SIGNS A CHILD MAY NEED COUNSELING

Counseling is a personal decision, and there's no hard-and-fast rule about when a child should or shouldn't see a counselor. If your child's feelings are interfering with day-to-day life, or you find yourself frequently wondering if counseling could help, that is reason enough to speak to a pediatrician or therapist.

William Worden, the psychologist behind the Harvard Child Bereavement Study, identified some warning signs that indicate a child is at higher risk and would benefit from therapy. They include:

* Being unable to talk about their loved one on an ongoing basis
* Serious, severe aggression or acting out
* Anxiety that gets worse instead of better over time
* Changes in eating or sleeping, or physical symptoms that don't go away
* Big, lasting changes in behavior, such as dropping out of activities or self-isolating
* Guilt that affects a child's self-esteem
* Suicidal thoughts or self-harm

Difficulty processing grief can also show up in a younger child's play. Play is how children learn, so acting out stories that relate to their loved one's death is usually a sign of a healthy response to grief. Occasionally, however, children who have lost a loved one in a frightening way may express trauma symptoms through post-traumatic play.

This style of play tends to be very repetitive and rigid and may act out events from the death in a literal way. Whereas healthy play tends to help children release emotions and self-soothe, this type of play often leaves children feeling more tense and agitated. Just like the symptoms mentioned previously, post-traumatic play is a good reason to speak to a pediatrician or counselor about grief therapy.

WHAT KIND OF THERAPY HELPS BEREAVED CHILDREN?

There are many therapy options available for grieving children, from peer support groups to family therapy to individual counseling. If you're beginning the search for a counselor, here are a few therapy approaches you can look for to ensure a good fit for your child:

* **Play Therapy:** Young children aren't developmentally ready to sit on a couch and verbalize their feelings to a stranger for an hour. Play therapy gives this age group an opportunity to use their actions, not their words, in order to express

themselves. Other creative therapies such as music, drama, and dance provide similar benefits.

* **TF-CBT:** If your child's loved one died in a very frightening way, they may be coping with the effects of trauma on top of their grief. They may have symptoms like intrusive memories, feeling on edge, or severe anxiety that get in the way of their healing. Trauma-focused cognitive behavioral therapy, or TF-CBT, was created to help kids dealing with trauma or traumatic grief. In this kind of therapy, kids and parents both learn skills to cope with trauma symptoms, and children can gradually work through their memories of the death so they no longer feel overwhelming.

* **Group Therapy:** A therapy group can be very validating for kids and teens, especially those who feel like nobody understands what they're going through. The National Alliance for Grieving Children and the Dougy Center are good resources for finding options in your state or town. Hospices, hospitals, and your child's pediatrician may also have recommendations for you.

MOVING AHEAD TOGETHER

Thank you for taking the time to learn about your child's experience with grief. Each moment that you have played, talked, and shared with your child has been time well spent.

In the middle of enormous pain and stress, you have taken a moment to try to see things through your child's eyes. By being open with your grief, you've helped your child know that they aren't alone, and that other people are thinking of and loving their special person too. You've given them the safe foundation they'll need to grow into healthy, thriving adults.

Bereaved children can and do thrive. Twelve former US presidents lost a parent as children or young adults. From judges to poets, scientists to actors, memoirs and biographies are filled with the stories of influential people who survived early losses. Grief may never fully leave us, but children can learn to live alongside it and create rich, meaningful lives.

RESOURCES

Brown, Laurie Krasny, and Marc Brown. *When Dinosaurs Die: A Guide to Understanding Death*. New York: Little, Brown, 2009.

Brown, Margaret Wise, and Christian Robinson. *The Dead Bird*. New York: HarperCollins, 2016.

Buscaglia, Leo. *The Fall of Freddie the Leaf: A Story of Life for All Ages*. New York: Henry Holt, 1982.

Cain, Barbara S., and Anne Patterson. *Double-Dip Feelings: Stories to Help Children Understand Emotions*. Washington, DC: Magination, 2001.

Cohen, Judith A. et al. *Treating Trauma and Traumatic Grief in Children and Adolescents*. New York: Guilford Press, 2017.

Docter, Pete, and Kemp Powers, dirs. *Soul*. Burbank and Emeryville, CA: Walt Disney Pictures and Pixar Animation Studios, 2020.

The Dougy Center for Grieving Children & Families. Accessed January 2, 2022. www.dougy.org/.

Haine, Rachel A. et al. "Evidence-Based Practices for Parentally Bereaved Children and Their Families." *Professional Psychology: Research and Practice*, US National Library of Medicine (April 2008). Accessed January 2, 2022. www.ncbi.nlm.nih.gov/pmc/articles/PMC2888143/.

Harris, Robie H., and Jan Ormerod. *Goodbye Mousie*. New York City: Simon & Schuster, 2004.

"How Do I Talk to My Children about Dying?" American Cancer Society. Accessed January 2, 2022. www.cancer.org/treatment/children-and-cancer/when-a-family-member-has-cancer/dealing-with-parents-terminal-illness/how-to-explain-to-child.html.

"How to Explain Suicide to Children and Young People." *Winston's Wish*, May 12, 2020. Accessed January 2, 2022. www.winstonswish.org/explain-suicide-to-children/.

"In Longest and Most Detailed Study of Pediatric Grief Following Parental Loss to Date, Department Researchers Find Increased Rates of Depression and Functional Impairment." University of Pittsburgh, Department of Psychiatry. Accessed January 2, 2022. www.psychiatry.pitt.edu/news/longest-and-most-detailed-study-pediatric-grief-following-parental-loss-date-department.

Institute of Medicine (US) Committee for the Study of Health Consequences of the Stress of Bereavement. "Bereavement During Childhood and Adolescence." In *Bereavement: Reactions, Consequences, and Care*, US National Library of Medicine. Edited by M. Osterweis, F. Solomon, and M. Green. Washington, DC: National Academies Press, 1984. Accessed January 2, 2022. www.ncbi.nlm.nih.gov/books/NBK217849/.

James, John W. et al. *When Children Grieve: For Adults to Help Children Deal with Death, Divorce, Pet Loss, Moving, and Other Losses*. New York: Harper, 2002.

Karst, Patrice, and Joanne Lew-Vriethoff. *The Invisible String*. New York: Little, Brown, 2018.

Katie, Byron, and Hans Wilhelm. *Tiger-Tiger, Is It True?: Four Questions to Make You Smile Again*. Carlsbad, CA: Hay House, 2021.

Kircher, Melissa. *The Endless Story: Explaining Life and Death to Children*. Scotts Valley, CA: CreateSpace, 2018.

Krulwich, Robert. "Successful Children Who Lost a Parent—Why Are There So Many of Them?" *NPR*, October 16, 2013. Accessed January 2, 2022. www.npr.org/sections/krulwich/2013/10/15/234737083/successful-children-who-lost-a-parent-why-are-there-so-many-of-them.

Levis, Caron, and Charles Santoso. *Ida, Always*. New York: Simon & Schuster, 2016.

Llenas, Anna. *The Color Monster: A Story about Emotions*. New York: Little, Brown, 2018.

Lowenstein, Liana. *Creative Interventions for Bereaved Children*. North York, Ontario, Canada: Champion, 2006.

Mellonie, Bryan, and Robert Ingpen. *Lifetimes: The Beautiful Way to Explain Death to Children*. New York: Bantam, 1983.

Molina, Adrian, and Lee Unkrich, dirs. *Coco*. Burbank and Emeryville, CA: Walt Disney Pictures and Pixar Animation Studios, 2017.

"Mr. Rogers Post Goes Viral." *PBS*, December 18, 2012. Accessed January 2, 2022. www.pbs.org/newshour/nation/fred-rogers-post-goes-viral.

Parr, Todd. *The Family Book*. New York: Little, Brown, 2010.

Pham, Steven et al. "The Burden of Bereavement: Early-Onset Depression and Impairment in Youths Bereaved by Sudden Parental Death in a 7-Year Prospective Study." *The American Journal of Psychiatry* 175, no. 9 (June 20, 2018). Accessed January 2, 2022. ajp.psychiatryonline.org/doi/full/10.1176/appi.ajp.2018.17070792?rfr_dat=cr_pub%3Dpubmed&url_ver=Z39.88-2003&rfr_id=ori%3Arid%3Acrossref.org.

Saks, Dan, and Brooke Smart. *Families Can*. New York: Penguin Random House, 2021.

Schwiebert, Pat et al. *Tear Soup: A Recipe for Healing after Loss*. Vancouver, WA: Grief Watch, 2018.

Seuss, Dr. et al. *My Many Colored Days*. New York: Alfred A. Knopf, 1996.

Silverstein, Shel. "Woulda-Coulda-Shoulda." *Falling Up*. New York: HarperCollins, 1996.

Thomas, Pat, and Lesley Harker. *I Miss You: A First Look at Death*. London: Wayland, 2021.

Tisdale, Sallie. *Advice for Future Corpses (and Those Who Love Them): A Practical Perspective on Death and Dying*. Melbourne, Australia: Allen & Unwin, 2018.

"What Is Cancer?" Reviewed by Dorothea N. Douglas. *KidsHealth*, Nemours Foundation, October 2016. Accessed January 2, 2022. https://kidshealth.org/en/kids/cancer.html.

Worden, J. William. *Children and Grief: When a Parent Dies*. New York: Guilford, 2002.

Worden, J. William. *Grief Counseling and Grief Therapy: A Handbook for the Mental Health Practitioner*. New York: Springer, 2009.

"Real Monsters." *ZestyDoesThings*. Accessed January 2, 2022. www.zestydoesthings.com/realmonsters.

INDEX